Teaching Young Children

about the author

Evelyn Beyer was born in Auburn, New York, and attended the University of Rochester, New York University, and the Bank Street College of Education, where she began to develop the approach to nursery school education that is embodied in this book. She has taught preschool children in New York and New Jersey, founded the nursery school at Sarah Lawrence College, was associated with the Mayo Clinic and has taught child study at Smith College. She is presently director of the nursery school and teacher at Sarah Lawrence College.

Teaching
Young Children

by Evelyn Beyer

PEGASUS   NEW YORK

Foreword

The United States Federal-supported Head Start programs for "disadvantaged" preschool children have captured the interest of many people. These children bring the impoverishment of their homes and neighborhoods to school. Because of their meager backgrounds, they begin primary school as potential failures, and often continue as failures until they drop out of the school system.

It has been heart-warming to observe the success of many of the Head Start programs. Children with a low estimate of their own worth have acquired skills and interests that have given them self-confidence. Their attitudes of suspicion and distrust have been changed to confidence in others and an eagerness to learn.

Nursery school education is now generally recognized as an essential part of the education of the individual. It is no longer the tolerated stepchild of the educational system. Nor is it considered merely a care-taking center for the children of working mothers, or a pleasant experience for a privileged few, or a precious research center for an even smaller group. It is now acknowledged as the first organized step which should be available to all children as they begin to climb the educational ladder.

In planning or assessing the nature of any preschool experience, it is tempting to focus on the program: what activities to plan, what materials to provide, what experiences to introduce between ten and ten-thirty. It is essential to recognize that what happens in a classroom is less important than the quality of the "happening"—that is, what it does to the child, and how he feels about it. The teacher is the crucial determinant of that quality. It is the teacher who creates the atmosphere and the attitudes toward learning that occur in the classroom.

This book attempts to describe the kind of person the teacher of young children needs to be: what she needs to know, what personal qualifications she should possess, what her teaching looks like, what it sounds like. The reader will see and hear children and their teachers as they relate to and learn from each other in the classroom.

If you are a parent wondering about what nursery schools are like, if you are a college student thinking about a career in nursery school teaching, or if you are an experienced nursery school teacher looking for refreshing ideas about nursery education, I hope you will find here some answers to your questions.

Bronxville, New York   E.M.B.

Acknowledgments

I wish to extend my gratitude to the pioneer teachers at the Bank Street School (long before it became a college), and to Jessie Stanton in particular, for having opened my eyes and ears to the lively signals about what they want to learn which young children give to perceptive adults. The early "researchers" at Sarah Lawrence College also deserve my gratitude. Lois Murphy, Joseph Stone, Mary Essex, and Eugene Lerner sharpened my awareness of the unique patterns in which children reveal their needs, their interests, and their self images.

I am grateful to the president of Sarah Lawrence College, Esther Raushenbush, for granting me time to assemble these thoughts about teaching young children. I also appreciate the patience shown by the teaching staff at the Sarah Lawrence Nursery School, who charitably endured my abstraction and my partial attention to their daily needs during this year of writing. I am especially grateful to the editing guidance of my "don," Madeleine P. Grant, who helped me to "tighten" the manuscript.

My final acknowledgment of gratitude goes forth to all the children I have ever taught. They have been my most vivid instructors.

Contents

Teaching
Young Children

One Day
in a Nursery School

A nursery school teacher brings her knowledge and understanding of the needs and interests of young children to her classroom. Even more important, she brings her own feelings. She brings herself. Believing in the importance of nursery school education as providing a solid base upon which subsequent learning experiences are built, she sees herself as a major influence in helping young children to gain confidence in themselves and in their ability to learn, and to trust and respect others.

She enjoys her teaching. She finds it stimulating and challenging. But our teacher is human, and some days are hard, physically and emotionally draining. She knows that her teaching is likely to be influenced by what happened before she comes to school: how she feels about the day, about the world, about herself, and even about the weather. Is she high or low in spirit? Is she feeling healthy, serene, and relaxed? Or is she feeling fatigued, uneasy, or tense? Is she worried about a personal problem? Has she had a refreshing weekend or a disappointing one? She knows that her ability to cope with these personal problems will influence the quality of her teaching.

One day in the life of a nursery school teacher seen through her eyes, her mind, her muscles, and her feelings will reveal some of the professional and personal demands made upon her.

Miss Bates teaches in a private, suburban, half-day nursery

school. It is housed in a spacious former residence suitably transformed for nursery school use. There are three groups in the school: the "elderly threes" (the youngest was three and a half at the beginning of the school year), a group of "young fours," and another of "older fours." Each group of fifteen children occupies a spacious, well-equipped room; each has its own toilet facilities and individual lockers for clothing. There is a kitchen which is shared for occasional group cooking projects, as well as for storage and preparation of the midmorning snack. There is also an attractive room for staff and parent conferences, and a modest office for the part-time secretary.

Most of the children are from middle-class, privileged families who can afford to pay the tuition. In addition, several children from lower income families have "scholarships" of reduced tuition. They are all bright children: responsive, imaginative, active, and eager to learn.

Each group has a head teacher and an assistant teacher. Student teachers from neighboring colleges participate as practice teachers, and student nurses from the local hospital attend as part of their pediatric training. Miss Bates teaches the "young fours," and she enjoys being a part of this congenial group.

As Miss Bates drives to school, she rehearses her plans for the day. It is going to be vegetable-soup-making day. She has brought the vegetables with her. She muses about which children will be attracted to the cooking venture. For those who are not interested, she will set up a table for sponge-painting. This requires little supervision, so she can focus on the "soup group." Then, of course, there will be the children who are regularly attracted to block-building or painting or puzzles. Probably the housekeeping corner devotees will be intrigued by the cooking project. She wonders about trusting Randy to use the vegetable scraper. Will he be challenged to master the technique of scraping, or tempted to use it as a weapon to poke and hurt someone? She decides to take the chance.

She arrives at school a half hour before the first child arrives. This gives her time to check on the consistency of the paints, to get out the brushes, to set up the sponge-painting table, and to prepare the juice trays. She smiles as she remembers that today there will be soup instead of juice, and she chooses saltines instead of the customary graham crackers. She decides against setting out the soup ingredients until after the children have arrived, so that she can talk about the project with them. She looks around the room with a glow of satisfaction. It is spacious, cheery, and attractive. It is well organized for good work and play, and it is ready for children. She feels a tingle of anticipation as she hears the footsteps and the voice of the first arrival. It is Beth, bursting with excitement and news. "You know what, Miss Bates? I growed!" Her mother follows, grinning. "She really has! We went to the doctor yesterday and he measured her. She has grown two inches since her last visit six months ago!"

Miss Bates smiles at Beth. "Beth, I'm sure you have grown. Perhaps we should make a marker and measure how tall everyone in this class is."

"First you have to make inches," adds Beth.

"We could borrow Mrs. Roach's yard stick," suggests Miss Bates, and stows away the idea as a good activity while the soup is cooking—a good opportunity to learn something about numbers and measurements.

Beth takes off her jacket, hangs it in her locker, kisses her mother goodbye, and discovers the sponge-painting setup. "I like this stuff," she says, "I can make spongy designs with it," and settles down to work.

The twins, Jeff and Teddy, are the next to arrive. They, too, have news that cannot wait. "Our guinea pig died, and Jeff cried, and we buried it in the ground and Daddy says we can get a new one and maybe a turtle, too!"

This is too much news to comment upon at the moment. But Miss Bates agrees that it is sad that the guinea pig died, that burying it was a good idea and that she is glad they were going to have a new one and also the turtle, adding that they could talk more about it later. They gallop over to Beth to repeat their story, then go to the block area to make a guinea pig house.

By this time children are arriving in groups. A car pool includes Tim, just back from a Florida vacation, Rick carrying a toy rifle nearly as large as himself, Sally with a cereal treat for the class, and Michael looking mad and reporting that Rick kicked him. Debby arrives with her mother, both looking as if they had been up all night. Suki and Lorna arrive holding hands announcing that they are inviting each other to their birthday parties, but not Debby or Beth. Suki's mother reports that Nels has the mumps, just as Randy tears into the room brandishing a rubber dagger.

Miss Bates welcomes Tim, tells him she has missed him and wants to hear about what he saw and did in Florida—but later. She reminds Rick to leave his rifle in his locker, thanks Sally for bringing the cereal treat, commiserates with Michael about the kick, and adds that she will talk with Rick about it. Beaming at Debby and her mother, she says, "You people look sleepy." She greets Suki and Lorna cheerfully, ignores their party threats for the moment, thanks Mrs. K. for the message about Nels, gives herself a reminder to tell Mrs. Roach, the secretary, to inform all parents in her group about the possible exposure to mumps, catches Randy in mid-swoop to discuss his rubber dagger.

Miss Gray, the assistant teacher, slips into the room, apologizing for being late, explaining that there had been a bad accident on the parkway and cars had been held up for miles. (Miss Gray is studying for her master's degree at a nearby college.)

Miss Bates gives her an understanding nod and returns to help Randy. She admits that rubber daggers couldn't really hurt or cut people, but that some children are frightened by them. She asks him to put the dagger in his locker, adding that as soon as all the children have arrived they are going to do something very special with *real* knives! She then reminds him that he might work on the airplane that he had started last week at the work bench. "I have found some wooden wheels that you could use for landing gear. Miss Gray could help you, if you need help," she tells him.

Randy considers these suggestions, slips the dagger into his locker, commenting, "But this couldn't really cut people." Then he asks, "Where are the wheels?" and scoots to the workbench.

David, Kurt, and Liza arrive. David has a new book about space. Kurt throws his hat into the room, runs across the floor, skids to a sliding stop, retrieves the cap, puts it on backwards and bursts into a giggle. Miss Bates notes his scattered entry, knows she must help him harness his cavorting spirits. "Hi, Kurt!" she says. "I'm glad to see you. When you get your jacket off, I have an important job for you to do."

She greets David, says his space book looks interesting and that she will look at it later.

She spies Liza lingering outside the door, peeking in, not quite able to make it. She goes to her, stoops down to Liza level, smiles at her, saying, "I'm glad you're here. I've been waiting for you. There is something new in the doll corner that I think you will like to see."

Liza enters slowly, edges toward the doll corner, smiles shyly as she spies the new tea set and the make-believe food. She fingers them tentatively, then begins arranging them on the table.

Kurt's mother rushes into the room. "I meant to warn you, Kurt is flying high today. His grandparents have just arrived from California. He is so excited, he is about to burst. If he can't settle down, telephone me and I'll pick him up early."

Miss Bates thanks her for the "fair warning," adding that Kurt has already demonstrated his high spirits, but that she hopes she can help him shift into lower gear.

She glances around the room. Everyone is busy, except Kurt who is waiting to hear about the important job. Suki and Lorna are painting with the pastel colors she had set out on the easel, still enjoying their "togetherness." "We are making spring pictures," announces Lorna. "With flowers and stuff."

"Mine is a spring design," adds Suki. "I like these milky colors."

"They are called 'pastels,'" Miss Bates tells her.

The sponge-painting table has several children dipping and printing. The block corner is bustling with building activity. Randy is hammering wheels on his airplane, Beth is working at a puzzle, David shows his space book to Liza. The hum of busy activity is a sound Miss Bates always loves to hear. She realizes that Robert is missing from the group and wonders whether yesterday's sniffles developed into something more serious. His mother will probably call to report.

"Now, Kurt, about that important job. We are going to make soup today and I need your help to start it. Will you please put these vegetables on the table while I get the scrapers?"

"*Real* soup?" asks Kurt.

"Real soup with real vegetables," answers Miss Bates.

"How do you make soup?"

"That's what we are going to find out about."

Kurt, who has simmered down from his bubbly entrance, dumps the vegetables in the middle of the table. Miss Bates places a bowl beside them. By this time several children have gathered around the table, curious about what is going on. Miss Bates has learned that with "young fours" she does not need to make a general announcement of a "community project"; individual children will be attracted to it—some to watch it, some to participate. Some will become absorbed and stay with it, others will drift in and out, others may ignore it altogether or give it only slight or passing attention. She knows that not *all* four-year-olds will necessarily be equally interested.

"We are going to make vegetable soup," she announces to the little group assembled around the table.

"Do you know what these things are called"? she asks, pointing to the vegetables in the middle of the table.

"Carrots!"

"Potatoes!"

"Onions!"

"Celery!" shout the children.

"Yes, they are all different kinds of vegetables," she agrees. "We are going to put them all in our soup. But first we have to fix them. We have to peel them and scrape them and chop them up. I have some scrapers and choppers. Randy, I thought you might like to try scraping. It's tricky to do. The scraper has a sharp scraping part, but it's not quite like a knife. Here, look at it."

Randy takes it, examines it, saying, "It's not sharp and pointy like a knife or a dagger."

"That's right," agrees Miss Bates, "but it does a good scraping job. I'll show you how it works." She holds a carrot by the stem and slides the scraper lengthwise. A long, skinny bit of carrot skin peels off.

"We can save the peels for the guinea pig," she tells them. "He will think they are delicious. Do you suppose we can scrape the potatoes? Let's try. They are harder to scrape because they are round. But how about peas and string beans? Can we scrape them?"

"No, you have to pop the peas out of their shells," says Suki.

"But you can't pop the beans," adds Beth.

"That's right," agrees Miss Bates. "Let's try snipping them with scissors. I'll cut the celery and onions, because this cutting knife is very sharp and I'm used to it."

"Yeah," says Kurt, "knives are dangerous. My mother says so. She says you can even cut an apple in two with them."

By this time several children are working, scraping carrots and potatoes. Randy skillfully and methodically peels long strips, Kurt attacks a potato with short jabbing scrapes, Suki and Lorna pop peas out of shells, Beth cuts string beans into pieces with scissors, commenting, "I help my mommy fix beans like this."

Miss Bates cuts the green onion into chunks, and the celery into small lengths. As potatoes and carrots become skinned, she cuts them up, adding them to the chopping bowl.

They talk about the smell and texture of the various vegetables. Miss Bates encourages nibbles. "Take a taste," she urges. "It's all right to eat raw vegetables. Some people like them better than cooked."

"Yeah, we have carrot sticks at home and celery, and you don't have to cook them; they're raw."

"What happens when you cook them?" asks Miss Bates.

"They get cooked," answers Tim.

"We'll see what happens when we cook these," says Miss Bates. "Do you know what we cook them in?"

"A pot with water," Beth answers. "That's what my mother does."

"Right," agrees Miss Bates. She fills a pot with water and sets it on the electric burner. "When it starts bubbling, it will be ready to put in the vegetables."

"Could I have a chopping turn?" begs Suki, taking the chopper and wielding it up and down in the wooden bowl. "Look, I'm chipping and chopping all these vegetables into nice little soupy bits."

Lorna reports, "The water is bubbling. It's ready for the vegetables."

David joins the group saying, "I'll put them in the water."

Taking the bowl of chopped vegetables, he dumps them into the water. The water stops bubbling. "Do you know why?" asks Miss Bates.

"Because the vegetables are sitting on top of the bubbles?" asks David.

"It seems like that," she replies with a smile, "but there is another reason. What happens when you put cold things into hot things? If you put some ice in hot water, what would happen, David?"

"The ice would turn to water; the hot would make it melt."

"Yes, but what would happen to the hot water; would it change"?

David is thinking hard. "It would get cooler."

"Right," agrees Miss Bates, "and that's what happened to our soup water. It was boiling, but the vegetables were cool, and when David dumped them in, they cooled the water so it stopped boiling. Let's watch and see what happens now."

"We forgot the peas!" reminds Jeff.

Miss Bates has a fleeting thought of suggesting that they add the peas later, preceded by a demonstration of the difference in texture between peas and root vegetables, but decides that there has been enough "vegetable teaching" for this session. She also decides to postpone discussion of how the different vegetables grow until another time. There has been enough talking. They dump the peas into the soup.

"My mother puts salt in her soup," adds Beth.

"That's a good idea. I think there is some in the kitchen, Beth. Will you please get it for us?"

Beth runs to the kitchen, Jeff gathers the peelings and pods to feed to the guinea pig, Miss Bates retrieves the scrapers, chopper, and the bowls. David still watches the pot. "It's beginning to bibbly, bubble a little," he announces.

"Then it's beginning to cook," adds Miss Bates.

"Here's the salt," calls Beth. "Could I shake it in?"

"First shake some in your hand so you can see how much. I think we need just a few shakes."

Beth shakes the salt and dumps it in the soup. "Now it will be flavory."

Miss Bates toys with the idea of adding a bouillon cube to make it more "flavory," but decides against it. This first "soup-making" needs to be focussed on the vegetables. The next time they might add stock or a soup bone or some canned tomatoes. So much to learn and to experience cannot all be absorbed in one cooking session!

The "soup-cookers" drift back to the activities they left before becoming involved in the cooking project.

Lorna and Beth join Liza in the doll corner. "We don't even have to fix make-believe soup, because we are making real live soup!" announces Lorna. The girls laugh, and Lorna adds, "I might even invite you to my birthday party, Beth."

Miss Bates smiles to herself. Apparently the soup-making has healed the birthday breach.

She glances around the room. Miss Gray has gathered a group of "loose-enders" around a table to play the new picture lotto game. Kurt, the "caller," enjoys the role and calls out, "Who has a monkey?"

"That's not a monkey; it's a chimpanzee," says Randy.

"A chimpanzee is the name of a flower!" says Kurt.

Miss Gray enters the discussion. She agrees that the picture card really is a chimpanzee, but adds, "I think Randy is thinking about the flower called 'pansy.' Listen to the sound of it: pansy, chim-panzee. Do they sound alike?"

"Yeah," Kurt agrees. "Pansy, the flower, and chimpanzee, a kind of monkey. That's funny."

"There are lots of words like that. Words that sound alike, but are really different. Can you think of some others?" urges Miss Gray.

"We play that game at home sometimes with my big brother," admits David. "Like 'lie' when you tell a lie, 'lie' when you lie down, and 'July' you know, in the summer."

Miss Bates turns her attention to the block area. The twins have switched from their construction of a guinea pig house to an airport for jets and helicopters, "so Tim can fly to Florida!"

"I'm already there!" admits Tim, "I just have to fly back!" Tim, constructing a pool, says, "The ocean is over here, but the waves are too high for the children."

Debby has lured Liza into the block area, "Let's build a

small house," she suggests, "one about *this* age," gesturing with her hand to indicate a moderate height.

Rick is building an intricate tower-like construction with unit blocks in a "cobb house" pattern. A cylinder tops it, arches curve outward at its base, colored cubes are inserted in the spaces between the blocks.

Miss Bates smiles as she views it, commenting, "That's a fancy high building you have made, Rick."

"I know it. It's a sort of a tower. But it's really for missiles and things. These are the lights," pointing to the cubes.

"That's interesting," replies Miss Bates. "You certainly have made it steady. I don't know much about missiles and things. David brought a book about space crafts. Maybe he has some ideas."

Sally, who had left her ornate block-building to kibitz on the lotto game, returns to find that the small wooden people she had placed around her building have been disarranged. "Someone has messed up my international relationships!" she protests. (Sally is the daughter of a United Nations official, so the comment is not surprising.)

Miss Bates smiles to herself; without commenting on the international aspects of the situation, she says, "I'm sorry your people got mixed up, Sally. I really don't know what happened to them, but I'll help to fix them up again, if you will show me where they go."

After helping to restore international relations she stands back, surveys the block area with a sense of satisfaction. How much these children have learned about using blocks since the beginning of the year! She rarely has to remind them to build away from the block shelves. The black tape floor boundary 12 inches from the shelf is a silent but effective reminder. They have also experienced the hazards resulting from building too close to the shelf: crashed buildings and hurt feelings.

Nor do they tend to assemble too many blocks before starting construction, blocks which obstruct and clutter. "Take two piles; then build with them. If you need more, take two more," had been her constant reminder. Miss Bates continues to pick up stray scattered blocks that don't seem to belong to any particular buildings, as well as accessories, cubes, cars, "people," that are lying around. These seem harder for children to see, and therefore often constitute hazards to the block community. Children stumble over them with consequent danger of building crashes.

She notes with interest that the children seem to be spacing their own buildings at safe, workable distances from each other. This, too, had been hard in the beginning. She remembers when she drew chalk-line boundaries on the floor to help them; "property lines" they called them. They did not have to be observed strictly, but they served as reminders of a building in process.

"I must get some new accessories," she thinks. Liza and Debby could use some squares of carpet or floor tiles for their "this age" house. She notes that the box of pieces of cloth needs replenishing. The block-building boys could probably use a box of assorted "tools" and gadgets; spools would be a good addition. Someone has mentioned a spool mill; perhaps she could beg a bag.

Just at that moment, when she is feeling so good about the activity in the block area, Michael whirls across the room with Randy's airplane aloft, aiming directly at Rick's tower, and lets it fly. It lands on target, and the tower crashes. Rick is startled by this totally unexpected and unprovoked attack. It was no accident! Rick rises from the shattered building with a scream of rage and lunges toward Michael with a block in his hand ready to avenge the attack. "You stupid Michael, you crashed my tower! You can't do that! I'm going to bomb you!"

Miss Bates manages to intercept the block bomb, holding Rick sympathetically but firmly.

"No, Rick, I can't let you throw the block. You want to hurt Michael because he crashed your beautiful tower. I'm sorry he did it, but I can't let you hurt him even though you want to. I'll help you talk with him. He needs to know it made you mad. And certainly we need to try to help him so he won't do things like that."

The comforting constraint of Miss Bates' arms, the reassuring words, the understanding feeling that she conveys, ease the tension of Rick's rage. He begins to cry, "Anyway he shouldn't do it, and he's stupid."

Michael ducks away from the scene and escapes into the safety of his locker.

Miss Bates and Rick walk toward him. Michael hides his face in his jacket. Rick lunges toward him, but again Miss Bates restrains him. "First, we have to talk with Michael. What do you want to tell him, Rick?"

"He shouldn't bust my tower!"

"Rick is right, Michael; he worked hard to build that tower, and then you wrecked it. That really was not such a good thing to do. It made Rick feel very angry. He wanted to hurt you, but I wouldn't let him, because I don't want you to be hurt. But I don't want you busting up other people's lovely buildings," says Miss Bates as she tries to reason and sympathize with both boys.

At this point Michael peeks out from behind his jacket. "Anyway Rick kicked me in the car."

Then Miss Bates remembers the early-arrival announcement about the kick.

"Is that why you crashed Rick's building? Oh, Michael, that doesn't help Rick not to kick you! I'm sorry we didn't talk about it sooner. And besides, throwing big airplanes inside the room is not a safe thing to do. It can only crash things or break things or hurt people. I'm going to try to help you so you won't do it again. It's dangerous.

"Michael, let's both of us help Rick pile up his blocks. There is still a little more work time, if you'd like to build another one. Let's see if Jeff and Teddy have room for that airplane in their airport. It needs to be in a safe place."

Michael remains in his cubby, not quite ready to accept the suggestion that he join the rebuilding project. Rick is still muttering, "He's stupid, that's what he is." Miss Bates squats down to help restore order to the shattered tower. As she piles the blocks, she talks with Rick.

"You are still mad at Michael, and I don't blame you, Rick. I guess he was remembering the kick you gave him. I have another idea: maybe we shouldn't have airplanes for indoor play. Or else we need a rule that says you have to hold the airplane in your hand while you pretend it is flying. That would be safer. What do you think, Rick?"

"Only it couldn't fly very fast in your hand."

"That's true. But it also couldn't crash into high towers like yours."

• "Yeah."

Just then there was a screech from David, "The soup! It's over-bubbling!" Miss Bates runs to lift the pot from the hot plate. Some of the liquid and bits of the vegetables have boiled over.

"It smells like burning," says Sally. "Like soup burning."

"It didn't really burn," replies Miss Bates, "but it did boil over. What do you suppose makes it do that?"

"It was *too* bubbly," says Tim.

"Because it got too hot," adds Jeff.

"Because there wasn't room in the pot for all those bubbles," said Beth.

"I think you are all right," said Miss Bates. "Let's take a little liquid out of the pot, and then we'll turn the heat down so it won't be quite so hot. Then it will cook more slowly with just little bubbles. That's called simmering, instead of boiling."

As the soup begins to simmer, children return to their other activities.

Miss Bates notices that Michael has emerged from his cubby and is hovering around the fringes of the housekeeping area. Beth has become the "mother," Liza is the "baby," and Sally the "big sister." They are absorbed in the dramatics of domestic roles. Beth is bossy but kindly as mother; Liza is placid and limp as a baby; Sally is a busy big sister. Michael, who had no official role, lurks around the edges.

Miss Bates takes in the situation at a glance, senses that Michael is headed for trouble or at least rejection by the female inhabitants. She decides to offer a suggestion that might ease him into the group. "Does this family have a daddy?"

Beth looks up from her ironing, spies Michael, senses the reason for the question, and answers, "Yes, but he's gone to the office."

"Oh," replies Miss Bates, "I just thought that this family might be able to use a man. Do you have any repairs that a man could do? Or do you need any deliveries of groceries or milk? Michael might be able to help you."

"I could wash the windows," suggests Michael.

(The housekeeping corner is actually in a corner of the room with two large windows of nine by twelve panes of glass.)

"OK, he could be the window-washer," grants Beth.

Michael beams.

"I have some real window cleaning spray stuff that you could use, Michael," adds Miss Bates. "You know, first you spray it on, then you rub it dry with paper towels."

"Yeah, I know," replies Michael, "I helped my mommy once to clean the low-down windows."

Miss Bates produces the spray, the paper towels, and even a window-cleaner's cap. Michael takes them to the housekeeping corner and enters triumphantly, chanting, "Window-cleaner, window-cleaner, here comes the window-cleaner man!" The ladies in the household acknowledge his presence with tolerant glances, then resume their play. But Michael is "in."

Miss Bates is pleased by the success and acceptance of her suggestion. She makes a mental note that she must do something toward providing more masculine accessories for the house-keeping area. "Daddies'" ties, vests, hats, and shoes were not enough. She decides that some discussions about what daddies do at home would be helpful; also discussions about workmen who come to the home, and the jobs they do. She is still thinking about these things, and noting that Michael is contentedly launched on his window-cleaning job, when Miss Gray whispers to her, "Where's Randy?"

A quick glance around the room reveals no Randy. Miss Bates notices that the rubber dagger is missing from his locker, and decides that Randy must have taken off with his trophy. She leaves the room in Miss Gray's charge, and goes across the hall to the group of "older fours." She checks with the teacher who has not seen Randy. She then goes to the room of the three-year-olds, and there is Randy sitting at a table with a mound of clay, stabbing at it with his dagger.

The teacher of the "threes" says, "I assumed this was a legitimate visit. Randy said you didn't mind. I must admit I've been too involved to check with you. I have no helper today."

Miss Bates thanks her for "taking care," tells her it is strictly an AWOL visit, and goes to Randy to discuss the situation with him. She approaches him very directly, but without anger or blame.

"Randy, we missed you. We didn't know that you had come to visit Miss Cook's group. You know, you must always tell us when you leave our room so we'll know where you are."

"Well, I needed to make a dagger dugout with clay," replies Randy.

"We have plenty of clay in our room. I think you just wanted to play with your dagger, and you didn't want me to see you."

At this, Randy covers his ears with his hands and shouts, "Shut up, you dirty rat! I won't listen to you!" Then he snatches the dagger from the clay "dugout" and darts from the room. Miss Bates follows swiftly, catching him just as he is about to open the door to escape into the playground. She holds him firmly as he struggles for release from her arms.

"Let me go, you rat!"

"No, I need to hold you, Randy. It isn't time to go outside now. I know you are pretty mad at me, and I guess I'm sort of mad at you, too. I don't like it when you run away from me and say mean words to me when I'm just trying to help you. We are going to stay here until you feel like coming back to our group. We still have work to do there. The soup is still cooking and we have to get things ready for our snack. I guess we'll have soup for juice today. Would you like to help me get things ready? We need some real cups instead of paper ones."

She feels his muscular tension relax. "Would you like to be the soup server?" Randy can't quite say "Yes," but he nods his acceptance, then asks, "How do I serve it?"

"With a ladle," answers Miss Bates. "That's a special kind of spoon. Let's go get it from the kitchen. I think the soup must be almost cooked. We'll test it."

"Test it?" questions Randy. "How do you test soup?"

"We'll taste it, and we'll stick a fork in the vegetables to see if they're soft."

"Oh," says Randy, "I never was a soup tester before."

Together they go to get the cups, the ladle and fork, and then return to the classroom for soup "testing" and tasting. The storm is over.

As they enter the classroom, "pick-up time" is already under way. Miss Bates gives Miss Gray a glance of approval. Beth has been placed in charge of tidying up the housekeeping corner. She is being somewhat managerial and bossy about it, but her helpers do not seem to mind. "The cups don't go *there,* they go on the cupboard shelf!" The block area is bustling. Miss Gray has obviously organized the putting away procedure. There are official "stackers" who arrange piles of similarly shaped blocks; there is a "shelf man." (Miss Bates notes that it is Kurt who seems to be enjoying this responsible position.) "Who has 'curvies'? I need 'longies.' Thanks a *lot,* Dave. That's a neat pile." Tim was collecting the wedgie "people," the cars, trucks, and assorted accessories. Each block has its replica in black silhouette taped to the shelf on which it belongs.

Miss Bates comments on the good job they are doing. "You block workmen are working so hard, and doing such a good job."

"Yes," replies Kurt, "we are neatening them up good."

"They look nice and neat," says Miss Bates, "but the really important thing is that you can see where everything belongs, and if you need a 'longie,' or a square or a triangle, you'll know where to find it. Right?"

"Right!" agrees Kurt, running his fingers over the smooth ends of the blocks.

Suki and Lorna are cleaning up the sponge-painting materials. Liza asks if she may wash the brushes.

As chores are finished, Miss Gray suggests that children needing to go to the toilet can do so. The bathroom is adjacent to the playroom, and these children are able to manage their own clothing and need no help with toileting. She also issues a reminder to rinse hands after their busy work time.

As the children complete this casual routine, they go to the book corner, select a book to look at while the snack "committee" prepares the tables.

In the meantime, Randy and Miss Bates have been tasting and "testing" the soup.

"We'll have to be careful, and not burn our tongues, Randy. It will be very hot."

"We could blow it," says Randy. "That's what my brother does. It makes it cooler."

"I'm going to put a little in a cup; that will get cool faster."

"Yeah," says Randy, "because it's not next to so much hot."

"That's right," agrees Miss Bates. "Now, would you please test the vegetables, Randy? Just poke the fork into the pieces of vegetable to see if they are soft or hard."

Randy pokes. The fork easily penetrates the vegetable bits.

"They are soft, all right," reports Randy.

"Good, then I think we can turn the heat off and take the pot off the hot plate. Now let's taste it."

They each spoon a taste from the cup.

"It's good. It tastes like soup, like real vegetable soup," they both agree.

"Would you like to serve it, Randy? It might be tricky, ladling it into the cups. Would you like to try it?"

"Sure," says Randy. "If it spills, I'll just sponge it up."

He works carefully spooning the soup into the cups on the tray. Miss Bates is impressed with his handling of the spoon, and his excellent hand-eye coordination.

"You certainly are doing a good job, Randy." And he knows he is.

Tim has already placed the paper napkins with two saltines on each one, and Debby has placed a plastic spoon at each place. Miss Gray arranges the tables into two groups, so that each set may have a teacher-hostess. Miss Bates carries the tray of soup to the tables and places a cup at each place; then grinning, she announces, "Soup's on!"

The children pile their books on the book shelf and dash for the tables. "I should have used the color game approach," thinks Miss Bates. "Red shoes, red shoes, come to the table. Walk on tiptoe if you are able"! She has collected several such chanting rhymes which children enjoy, as aids in avoiding a chaotic free-for-all rush.

The novelty of "soup for juice" seems to provide its own built-in controls. The children select their own places, sit down with minimal jostling, without arguing about who will sit next to whom. The soup is the focus of interest.

"I'm going to tell my mother we had real live soup for juice, and we even made it," comments Beth.

"With vegetables," adds Tim.

"How does it taste?" asks Miss Bates.

"Like vegetable soup!" answers David. "I can taste the onions and the celery."

"I can smell the onions!"

"The vegetables got all mooshy."

"Do you know why?" asks Miss Bates.

"Because the water got into them and softened the hardness, and the cooking did it," adds Randy.

"That's a very good explanation, Randy," comments Miss Bates.

"But where are the peas?" asks Rick.

"Maybe they got too mooshy and just mooshed up to little green pieces," explains Michael.

"No, I ate one and it wasn't even crunchy like the carrot or the potato!" says Lorna.

"Well, maybe that's why it cooked up softer."

"What do you know about carrots and potatoes?" asks Miss Bates. "You have said they are both hard before they are cooked. What else is alike about them? Do you know how they grow?"

"They are not the same color," replies David. "You know carrots are sort of orangy and potatoes are brown on the outside but white on the inside."

"That's right, David. Are they the same shape?"

"Oh, no. Carrots are skinny, and potatoes are roundy."

"Does anyone know how they grow?"

"From seeds. My daddy planted some once and after a long time they grew," announces Suki.

"Do you remember how they grew?" asks Miss Bates.

"Yes. It was funny because the carrots were in the ground and we had to pull them up. The fuzzy green was on top."

"You are right," agrees Miss Bates. "Carrots are root vegetables. They grow in the ground. Potatoes do too. How about peas and celery?"

"I don't think they grow under the ground. I think they are on top, but I'll ask my daddy," adds Michael.

During this vegetable discussion, children spoon the soup and munch their crackers.

"I think this soup is delicious," adds Lorna, "and I'm going to tell my mother the recipe."

"What is a recipe?" asks Tim.

"It's how you cook something," replies Lorna.

"We forgot my treat!" squeals Sally.

"We were so busy making our soup, we forgot," agrees Miss Bates. "Would you like to serve it now, Sally?"

"Yes, it could be for dessert, it's sugar pops." She spoons a serving into each child's hand.

Most of the children thank her. Miss Bates issues a general thanks. "Thank you, Sally. It was kind of you, to bring a special treat and share it with us. Now, will those who are finished with soup and treat, please put napkins in the wastebasket, cups on the tray and join me in the story corner."

There is a mild scramble as the children place cups on the tray, napkins in the wastebasket, and scurry to the story corner. Miss Bates sits on a child-size chair. The children gather around her on the floor. There is some crowding and jostling, but no major conflicts. Miss Bates begins singing, "Here we are together, together, together. Here we are together, all sitting on the floor. There's Suki and Lorna and Michael and David (naming and pointing to each child) all sitting on the floor."

"Who is not here today?" she asks.

"Nels, because my mommy says he has the mumps."

"That's right," agrees Miss Bates. "I think it would cheer Nels if we sent him a letter or some cards or pictures. Would you like to do that? You could tell me what to write."

"You could write, Dear Nels, we are sorry you have mumps. Do they hurt? We miss you. Love. . . ."

Beth is an old hand at dictating letters. She is the self-appointed class social secretary. Everyone agrees it is a good idea to send a letter to Nels.

"We could tell him we made soup today," adds Kurt.

"And we could tell him our guinea pig died," adds Teddy. Miss Bates has been scribbling notes of these suggestions.

"Tomorrow, during work time, I'll write the letter, and people who would like to make pictures could do that, and then we'll put them all in an envelope for Nels."

"But don't forget the stamp," adds David.

"You are right, David. We always have to put a stamp on the envelope when we mail a letter. Do you know why?"

No one has an answer to that question, and Miss Bates realizes it is probably beyond their comprehension.

"We might take Nels' letter to the post office. Perhaps the post office man could tell us why letters need stamps."

"Or my daddy might know," adds Jeff.

Miss Bates smiles. Daddies are often the ultimate sources of all knowledge to four-year-olds. She isn't sure how much her "fours" would get from a post office trip, but she thinks it may be worth trying. At least they could observe the process by which a letter starts on its way.

"I wonder why Robert isn't here. If he has a cold, we could send him a letter, too, and mail it with Nels'." They all agree.

Thoughts of observing the mail process are speeding through her head as she prepares to read the story she has selected. She has chosen to read *The Dead Bird* by Margaret Wise Brown. There has been a lot of talk about death and dying lately (Rick's grandfather had died earlier in the school year) and the death of the twins' guinea pig makes it seem like a good choice.

"Is everyone comfy?" she asks. "This is a story about a dead bird," she begins.

"The bird was dead when the children found it."

She holds the book so all the children can see the full page picture of the children finding the dead bird. She continues to read the story.

The children listen attentively; the twins are especially absorbed. Several times they interject:

"That's what you are s'posed to do, dig a hole in the ground."

"Only we put our guinea pig in a shoe box first."

"We didn't sing a song; we just said, 'We'll miss you, Guinea.'" Miss Bates turns to the last page and reads, "And every day until they forgot, they went and sang to their little dead bird and put fresh flowers on his grave," adding, "And that's the end of the story."

The last picture shows the bird's grave in the woods, and on the opposite page, a drawing shows the children playing ball.

There is an audible sigh of seeming contentment and approval.

"Read it again," says Rick.

Miss Bates smiles, saying, "I will read it again some other day, Rick. We need to go outside. But I'm glad you like it."

"Did you know my grandfather died? And they buried him just like a bird," adds Rick.

"I know," admits Miss Bates.

"And I miss him, too."

"I'm sure you do, Rick."

Miss Bates slips her arm around his shoulder, saying, "It makes us feel sad, when people that we love die. But we keep remembering them."

"Yeah," adds Rick, "until we forget."

"That's right," and she recalls the author's final sentence: "And every day, until they forgot. . . . ," and she knew how truly childlike it was. It is good to mourn, but it is natural to forget; good to grieve, but then to return to play.

Children begin donning jackets preparatory to going outside. They are all rejoicing in the warmth of spring, and the release from the nuisance of snow pants and mittens and scarves and boots and caps. The day before they had chanted their delight: "no more snowsuits, no more snowboots, no more mittens!"

Today Miss Bates begins singing, "What shall we do when we go outside, go outside, go outside? What shall we do when we go out to play"?

"Swing," suggests Sally.

"Sally will swing on the swinging swing, swinging swing, swinging swing; Sally will swing on the swinging swing, when we go out to play."

"I'm going to dig in the digging place," adds Kurt.

"Kurt will dig in the digging place, digging place, digging place; Kurt will dig in the digging place when we go out to play."

"I'm going to build a space ship," says David.

"David will build with the blocks and boards, blocks and boards, blocks and boards, David will build with the blocks and boards when we go out to play."

By this time everyone is ready, and they troop outside into the spring sunshine. Miss Bates is pleased to see that the horizontal ladder has been mended, and the sand box has been replenished with mounds of fresh sand.

Teddy, Tim, and Rick are attracted to the sand box. "We could make roads and stuff. Get the dump trucks, Ted, and shovels!" Ted trots off to the toy shed, seemingly pleased to be selected as errand boy by Rick. The three of them become absorbed in a major construction project. Debby and Liza approach the sand box, not quite sure of the reception they may receive from the road construction gang. Miss Bates watches, hoping they will assert themselves, but ready to help them if they need support. As they continue to watch, she tells them, "I think there is room in the sandbox for you two. Would you like to help the road-builders?"

"No, we just want to make cupcakes," Debby replies.

"Oh, that's easy," says Miss Bates, drawing a line through the sand marking a corner space. "This could be the cupcake-making place." Then she alerts the boys to the situation. "Road-builders, be careful when you come to this part of the sandbox; Debby and Liza are going to be making cupcakes." "OK," answers Tim.

Miss Bates glances around the playground. Sally and Beth are swinging. She notices that Beth has mastered the skill of "pumping." Sally is working at it, but hasn't quite mastered the rhythm.

Randy is working hard to "skin the cat" on the horizontal bar. He has already succeeded in a front somersault. Miss Gray is standing nearby, ready to help, offering encouragement.

Jeff, Suki, and Norma are setting up a construction of aluminum ladders, gangplanks, boards, sawhorses. It becomes quite intricate and attracts several children who use it for climbing, sliding and bouncing. Miss Bates is confident that they can manage the situation. She tests a few of the boards and ladders to be sure they are securely attached, and at one point, when children seem to be approaching the set-up from two directions, she suggests a one-way traffic approach. "Then there won't be collisions. You might even need a traffic policeman, or a traffic light."

"Yeah, I'll be the cop!" offers Jeff.

Miss Bates notices that Jeff is climbing with much more confidence than he had shown earlier in the school year. He is now able to climb to the top, and slide down the shute without holding onto the sides. She has also watched him observing Nels as he hangs by his hands from the horizontal ladder and then

"walks" across by his hands. Jeff had seemed to be admiring Nels' feat, and also to be studying the technique. She had a feeling he would soon be ready to try it himself.

Kurt and Randy are digging in the digging place, using sturdy trench shovels. "We're going to dig a dam," announces Kurt. "If we dig deep enough, we might find a Chinese worm," from Randy.

Miss Gray smiles, deciding not to interrupt the digging project with a discussion of the nationality of worms, or the likelihood of reaching China. "Could you use a wheelbarrow to haul your dirt away?" she asks. "Not yet," answers Kurt, "we have to dig deeper."

The builders, under David's leadership, are launched on their spaceship construction. David is clearly the boss and a well-informed one. He knows his spaceship facts, and his helpers respect his knowledge. Miss Bates realizes that he probably knows more than she does about space craft. Wishing she had read the book he brought, she reminds him that they hadn't had time to look at his book.

"That's OK," answers David, "I will tell you about it tomorrow." Then turning to his fellow astronauts he suggests, "We need two more blocks to cover the hatch," and his co-pilots scurry off to get them.

Miss Bates wonders how they will manage to lift off, but then realizes this will be no problem. Their imagination will carry them aloft after the count down, which David has already mastered. Could he count "up" as well as down? she wonders.

She notices Liza and Debby creeping along the stone wall, each with a pail in hand. They have abandoned the cupcake-making project; apparently the road-builders were a little too threatening.

"We're looking for spring," announces Debby.

"What a good idea," answers Miss Bates. "I'd like to see what you find."

Lorna's mother comes into the yard to pick up Lorna and Suki. She apologizes for being a little early, explaining that she needs to go to the city. Lorna is to have lunch with Suki. This is an exciting prospect for both little girls, and takes the edge off the pain of early departure.

"But we didn't even have music today," claims Suki.

"You are right, Suki," answers Miss Bates. "We were so busy with our soup-making, we didn't have time. But tomorrow we will have a long music time. Kate is bringing her guitar."

"Good," says Lorna, "see you tomorrow. Goodbye, Miss Bates, goodbye, Miss Gray," and off they go hand in hand.

"Goodbye, friends," replies Miss Bates, "have fun. See you tomorrow."

Other mothers begin arriving. Kurt's mother asks, "How did things go? Did he simmer down?"

"Oh, yes," answers Miss Bates. "After the 'slide-in' arrival, he quieted down. Our soup-making captured his interest and a deep digging engineering project harnessed his energy."

"Hooray for soup and digging."

Rick's mother asks if the rifle had caused any trouble.

"Not directly," answers Miss Bates, "however, I think it might be safer to leave it at home. It can be a potential source of trouble in a group. Rick and Michael had a minor battle this morning. I don't think the rifle triggered it. But it's a threatening weapon, even in a locker."

"I'm sure you are right. I was in a hurry this morning and too soft-hearted to insist that Rick leave it at home."

Randy comes racing up to Miss Bates. "Where's my dagger? You said you would keep it safe."

"And I did," answers Miss Bates. "It's safe in my pocket, and here it is," she answers, handing it to him, smiling. "We had a little trouble with it, didn't we, Randy?"

Randy grins, "Yeah, but—"

"Yes, but you were a good soup taster and tester, weren't you?"

"Yes," agrees Randy. "And you know what? I want to whisper something." Miss Bates leans down. Randy whispers, "You really aren't a dirty rat."

"Thanks a lot, Randy. That makes me feel cheery." Miss Bates smiles and gives him a quick hug before he gallops off with his mother.

Beth runs up to Miss Bates, "We forgot to measure our inches!"

"You're right, Beth. It was that soup that kept us so busy.

Will you remind me to do it tomorrow? Perhaps your mother has a yardstick that we could borrow. Would you ask her?"

"Could I leave my building up?" asks David. "The spacecraft isn't quite finished."

"Surely," answers Miss Bates. "And I'm going to learn more about these things."

"You could borrow my book if you'll bring it back tomorrow."

"Thanks a lot, David. That should really help me."

Most of the children have left. Debby and Liza are still hunting for spring when Debby's mother arrives.

"Debby seemed a little droopy today," Miss Bates tells her.

"I probably should have kept her home," answers Mrs. T. "We were both up half the night with stomach upsets. She seemed to feel all right this morning, and she was so eager to come, I couldn't bear to keep her home. I must admit I slept all morning."

"I think your first thought was probably the wise one. But she seems to have survived the morning. She is now hunting for spring."

The two little girls approach with their sand pails. "We didn't find much spring," admits Debby. "Only a bird feather, a worm, two buds and some green stuff like grass only it smells like onions. We couldn't find pussywillows."

"Maybe next week we can find some more. I know where some violets grow, and forsythia bushes should soon be blooming. We'll go hiking and look for spring."

The last child and parent have left. Goodbyes have been said; assorted reminders have been delivered. Now the teachers can sit down to share their impressions of the morning. Miss Gray gathers up stray shovels and pails and trucks to put in the toy shed.

They return to the playroom, which seems in good order. The sponges and the soup pan are soaking separately. Miss Gray gives the paint brushes an extra swish, and covers the paint jars. The block area is all set; the housekeeping corner has a few stray articles to be put in place. This has been a day of minor spills, so tables need minimal sponging.

As the teachers complete these end-of-morning chores, they talk about the morning's highlights.

"Well, the soup seemed successful," comments Miss Gray.

"Yes, I felt it was," replies Miss Bates. "I hope I didn't over-do the vegetable discussion. I know I left a few loose threads. Carrots may come from seeds, but potatoes come from pieces of potatoes, right? I wasn't very bright. I should have reminded them of our sweet potato, but maybe that would have been confusing."

"We could read the *Carrot Seed* story again," suggests Miss Gray.

"Yes, I thought of that, but somehow 'death' seemed more urgent today."

"I agree. They certainly listened attentively to that story."

"Randy had a tough time, but I think it turned out all right. He certainly gets furious when he can't do what he wants to do. But I think he is doing better. He can listen, and he can respond to suggestions. Today the speed of his switch from rage at me to a willingness to assist in the soup testing and tasting was a great improvement. Earlier in the year he would have sulked for a long time and resisted any suggestion of returning to the group.

"I'm not sure I did as well with Michael. He acts so swiftly. I really didn't anticipate that airplane crash into Rick's tower. And I'm afraid Rick wasn't satisfied with the way I tried to help them."

"What about Liza"? asks Miss Gray. "It's so easy to forget about her. She is so undemanding, so unassertive."

"Well, she got chosen to be Beth's baby, and this may have been good for her. I have a hunch that her mother may be putting a lot of pressure on her to grow up, maybe a little more than she can take. I must have a conference with her soon."

"I don't think Liza is terribly unhappy. She just doesn't seem to have much confidence in herself. This is the kind of child that probably needs to be the object of a campaign of approval. Not a barrage of artificial compliments, but casual comments of genuine approval. Let's make an effort to notice the things she does well or enjoys doing, and let her know that we notice them."

"It probably wouldn't hurt to have a similar campaign of reporting to Liza's mother. We need to try to change Liza's picture of herself into one that convinces her that people value her, but we also need to help her mother to recognize that we see Liza as a competent little girl.

"It was a good morning," adds Miss Bates.

"We will be discussing aggression in my course this afternoon. I'll have some good examples to report," says Miss Gray.

"All kinds," agrees Miss Bates. "Verbal, physical, subtle, overt. These children really speak and act out their feelings. They haven't learned to disguise them. I love their directness. It is refreshing. You seldom have to wonder what they are thinking and feeling. Have a good class; see you tomorrow."

After Miss Gray leaves, Miss Bates sits down to write a few brief notes. She keeps a log of outstanding events of each morning: new trends or developments or responses of individual children. She also keeps a card file of anecdotes, which she finds helpful in discussing children with parents or with students.

She is having an orientation meeting this afternoon with a group of student nurses who will be observing and participating in the nursery school for the next month. She enjoys these sessions. Sometimes it is hard to help them to "see" children and to listen to them. They are so accustomed to doing things for sick children. A month is a short time, but the experience is an intensive one. She always hopes they will be better nurses of sick children as a result of this experience with well children.

She leaves the room to visit with the other teachers, and to hear about their morning experiences. She is glad to be the teacher of her group, and smiles as she enters Miss Lane's room. "Here comes a dirty rat!" she announces. "I mean I *used* to be, but I'm not any more. Randy said so, and *he* knows!"

A Place to Play

Our morning visit in Miss Bates' classroom revealed that play was its central and consuming activity.

Current concern about the importance of cognitive learning, and the tendency to push even young children into readiness for academic achievement, forces teachers and directors of nursery schools to emphasize the value of play for young children, for it is one of the most important experiences in their intellectual and emotional development.

We need to realize first, that adult ideas about play are very different from those of young children. Adults turn to play as a well-earned reward after a spell of hard work. It may be relaxing, it may be physically exhilarating; but it is separate from work. Play for a young child *is* his work—his education, as well as his fun.

When parents plan for play for their children, too often they arrange it to meet their own convenience. Children playing contentedly are occupied and quiet. Mother is free to go about her household business, and household work is foremost on her mind.

Some homes provide a special playspace, a room or a corner of a room where the child is supposed to play. Sometimes these areas are stocked with intelligently selected toys that hold the interest and absorb the energy of children. More often they are a clutter of inappropriate toys just waiting to be broken or ignored. Sometimes they are stocked with so many toys, they only bewilder the child.

I have heard mothers say, "I can't understand why Joel won't play in his playroom. It's full of every kind of toy I can think of. But he seems to prefer playing with my pots and pans, or with water in the sink." These mothers do not realize that pots and pans and water are important play material to young children. They prefer them to many more elaborate commercial toys. They also like being with mother doing what she does, rather than being alone in a playroom.

I have watched a young father eagerly instructing his three-year-old son in the skills of pitching a ball, only to observe his irritation with the child's awkward movements. At three it is enough that the child be able to roll or toss a ball in the general direction of a catcher. His muscular coordination is not sufficiently developed to meet his father's overeager expectations. By six or seven, his muscles will be ready to profit from his dad's instructions, and then he can and will want to follow them.

Families with young children living in small apartments with limited space for play, must cope with the problem of having children underfoot. For these families the nursery school is a delight: a place organized and equipped to meet the needs of young children. At nursery school, play is the core of the curriculum, not just because children at play seem contented and happy and busy, but because play is the medium through which they learn so much.

For young children, play is not a casual pastime. It is the joyous *work* of childhood.

Dorothy Weisman Gross, of Brooklyn College, describes play as "the beautiful central fact of childhood. Through it a child may strengthen his growing powers, may express his deepest feelings, may comfort himself, may discover and explore the paradoxes of the world and of himself. . . ." She adds, "For it is through play that a child may find his own unique connection with the world he was given. It is not 'only' play, but also the most important business a child has. . . ."[21]

Lawrence K. Frank (lecturer, consultant, author) wrote, "Play is the way a child learns what no one can teach him."[21]

Barbara Biber (Distinguished Research Scholar, Bank Street College of Education) defines play as a "growth process." She describes the play of young children as having, "the quality of an intense, absorbing experience."[10]

These experts have watched young children at play and know its importance in the growth of the child. What they have to say in defense and in praise of play has helped nursery school teachers provide richer opportunities for meaningful play in the classroom.

The way the teacher sets the stage will influence the kind of play that occurs. The way she organizes the space and selects the materials will determine the quality of play. She knows that toys are tools that may stimulate or block good play, but toys must also be of good quality. Poorly constructed, easily broken ones, however glamorous in appearance, are an obstacle to good play experiences. Wind-up toys that wiggle or jump or squeak invite only passive observation before their untimely demise. The child is left with nothing to do but look at them until the mechanism gives out, and that usually happens soon.

The teacher is aware of the range of play activities that involve children's minds and muscles, and she provides for them accordingly. Much of young children's play is physical activity. Part of this may seem like an overflow of undirected energy and exuberance, but much of it is the necessary process by which muscular learning takes place. It is hard for adults to realize that children have to learn to run, skip, hop, and jump, climb and balance. Space and suitable equipment are needed for the practice and development of these skills, and the good nursery school provides them.

Children need a variety of play materials which they can manipulate with their hands. Barbara Biber wrote, "There is pleasure and satisfaction in what one's hands can make of the physical world, and the child, in his playful remaking of the world around him, lays the cornerstone of his feelings about himself in relation to that world."[10]

These hand-manipulated materials are the "raw materials": paints, clay, dough, paper, crayons, blocks. Using them promotes discoveries of texture, color, pattern, design, shape. As the child plays he brings himself and his ideas to them, and creates something uniquely his own. He also learns the different qualities of these materials, the range of exploration they provide, and he discovers their limits. He is challenged to think through their appropriate uses: how to build a tower that will not topple; how to shape a dinosaur from clay; how to keep colors separate on his painting paper.

Some play materials do not invite multiple choices of discovery, but a single one. Inset puzzles, which are examples of this latter kind, permit only one correct way of completing the puzzle. This type of challenge is favored by the Montessori method of teaching, and these so-called "didactic materials" are designed to teach specific relationships of color, size, shape, number, texture, volume, etc. They must be manipulated in one way only. Specific problem solving tasks have genuine appeal for many children, and when used in conjunction with "raw" materials, provide a variety of learning experiences. A fuller discussion of this type of material appears in a later chapter on the Montessori method.

Some materials, such as blocks, stimulate the child's imagination and foster dramatic play. The child who brings to blocks the idea of creating a firehouse which he then constructs is seldom content to leave it at that. A fire house must have fire engines and firemen, and there will surely need to be a make-believe fire to be put out!

In the early days of nursery education, few toys other than the strictly "raw" materials were used to stimulate dramatic play. There were a few bleak stand-up rubber dolls, and a box of "covers" near the block shelves. Sometimes there were interlocking block trains. There were no "doll corners" which today are filled with child-size, housekeeping furnishings: dress-up clothes (male and female), cooking utensils, dishes, purses, suitcases, mops and brooms, all suggesting dramatization of the familiar. Some educators criticize the richness of these housekeeping areas: they claim that they are so realistically furnished, that nothing is left to stimulate the child's imagination. However, the child brings his imagination to a situation, and will utilize the props he finds there to fit his own dramatic plan. He improvises: "The baby is sick; we need a thermometer. I know, we can use a stick."

Other critics of these doll corners object to their predominantly female character. They are, to be sure, happy havens for
little girls to be mothers, and to carry on all the delights of
domestic dramatizing. They cook, they serve dinner, they put
the baby to bed, they telephone, they go marketing. But there
is not much for "daddies" to do. Teachers often make ardent
pleas for "daddy dress-up clothes," ties, shoes, vests, hats. Often
little girls take over the doll corner completely and manage to
exclude all males. They may tolerate an occasional "doctor" or
"repair man" or "delivery man." One teacher provided a bat-
tered typewriter and an attaché case for the office-bound "daddies." But I think the critics are justified in feeling that we
have not discovered the male equivalent of the predominantly
female doll corner.

Of course, dramatic play often goes on without the aid of specially designed props. A four-year-old who needs to be a cat
doesn't need whiskers or a tail! And the four-year-old who
needs to be a lion has his own built-in roar which he can turn
on at will.

Dramatic play gives young children a chance to act out, to
dramatize some of their strong feelings. They can *be* the cross
mother, or the big bad wolf, or Batman, or the helpless baby
and it's all right. Children are actually helpless and powerless
in the well-ordered adult world which controls them, but in play
they find release from feelings of helplessness by dramatizing the
sense of power they crave. *They* can be the big guys, and even
the *bad* guys.

Some of the conversations overheard in dramatic play reveal
the kinds of concerns and confusions children have.

Four-year-old Andrew was rolling a snake out of clay. "I'm
making a big snake! The snake says, 'I'm being made by God
on his operating table!' I'm God. I'm making big snakes, I
make the world! This big snake is a huge boa constructor. He's
coiling. He's a black cobra. Isn't he huge? I've seen them in
the zoo coiling from here to here. I'll take him home and have
him bite every one in the family—even Grammy and Grampy.
I'll put him on the terrace and I'll say, 'Look at the big, black
cobra!' and I'll fool 'em! I'm God all right!"

Andrew's message was rather clear. He needed to feel that

he was controlling some of the power assigned to God. By creating a clay cobra and talking about his wishes to "bite everyone in the family, even Grammy and Grampy," he could be painlessly relieved of his hostile wishes without harming anyone.

Dramatic play, whether with clay, dress-up clothes, blocks, wheel toys, or puppets, is an important way for children to express their inner needs and feelings, as well as their ideas. Such play reflects the events or relationships they have experienced. By imitating daddy, mommy, baby, the fireman, the policeman, or the "fix-it" man, the child reveals his understanding, as well as his confusions, about their roles.

Sometimes this playing out of roles is more than a casual imitation of the person or the experience; it may also reflect strong feelings related to significant persons or events. A timid child may assume the role of the dominating parent, and treat the baby harshly. The child who is being pressed to be more grown-up may retreat into the comfort and safety of the baby role. In dramatic play, children may express impulses and needs that are not accepted in the real life situations. Such play provides release and relief to the child. Erikson states that the child uses play "to make up for defeats, sufferings and frustrations"[17] he meets in everyday living.

Susan Isaacs points out that dramatic play not only helps the child understand the behavior of things and people, but when the child plays at being father, mother, baby, giant and giant killer, wild animal and hunter, he is "externalizing his own inner drama."[25] In dramatic play the child expresses his fantasies and thereby eases his own inner tensions. Susan Isaacs also states that this easing of tension results in a "new equilibrium of mental health, and happiness is attained."[25]

Hartley, Frank and Goldenson state that dramatic play is "the means by which the child works out his difficulties for himself, so that he can meet the challenge of his world with confidence."[22] They refer to the three motifs which occur over and over again in the dramatic play of young children: the need for protection (for mothering, babying, being cared for), the need for power (over things and people), and the need to attack and destroy.

From observing children's dramatic play, teachers can learn much about the concerns of these children. "Dramatic play reflects not only the flavor of the child's life, but the needs which his experiences generate."[22] Observation of children's dramatic play may reveal "a great deal about the relationships, people, needs and impulses that preoccupy them."[22] It also gives us clues concerning the child's ideas and feelings about himself, and what others think of him.

Sometimes it is difficult to distinguish between play which is a projection of actual situations and that which is an expression of the hopes and wishes of the child. Often these two facets are combined in dramatic play. The teacher needs to be cautious about attaching deep significance to any single episode. But she will be alerted to recurrent themes in dramatic play of individual children, which may be clues to a better understanding of the child and his needs.

Sand, mud, water, finger paint are important play materials which educate the sense of touch. Some children who have been conditioned against getting dirty are reluctant to handle them; they cannot take a risk that might get them into trouble. Children who are free to explore, delight in the slurpiness of mud or finger-paint. Water, just plain water, is a play material that offers hours of relaxed contented play. Pitchers, funnels to pour into, egg beaters, soap flakes, and detergents to make suds, sponges to squeeze, boats to float, straws to blow bubbles, all provide fun for young children. A child-height sink is desirable, but a basin of water at a table, or a tub of water around which plastic-aproned children may gather is equally satisfying. And things to scrub: doll clothes, dishes, cups, pans, table tops. One teacher let children take turns washing the windows with a spray-on cleanser followed by vigorous wiping. This was a favorite activity. It was play—but it was *work,* and it was *real!*

Children sometimes need the comfort of cuddly animals. Although they may lose interest in this kind of play material as they reach out for new experiences, it is good to have a cuddly something on hand for a child when he needs it.

People often ask, "but don't you play *games* in the nursery school? Or is it all just free play?" Yes, there are simple group games that young children can play and enjoy. There are the commercial picture lotto games, picture domino games, and giant dominoes with color dots that can be matched.

Then there are various simple guessing games. "What did I take away?" is a favorite. The teacher places a number of familiar objects collected from the room in a circle. The children examine and identify them. One child shuts his eyes while one of the objects is taken away. The child opens his eyes and tries to remember the missing object. All kinds of variations of this can be played with colored cubes or various lengths of sticks as well as a miscellany of objects. Hiding games, of objects, or children are also fun. A child is chosen to hide and has to be identified by the child who has closed his eyes. The "feely" game, reaching in a sack and identifying the enclosed object by feeling it, is another favorite.

Older four-year-olds enjoy dramatizing familiar stories. "How Spot Found a Home" in *The Here and Now Storybook* by Lucy Sprague Mitchell and "Hurry, Hurry" by Edith Thatcher Hurd are favorites. The children will enjoy improvising simple props and stage settings. Costumes are not essential except perhaps for a tail for Spot, the Cat. The teacher may read the story as the children provide the dramatization, or the children may do it by themselves. There is no need to memorize the lines. An "audience" composed of the non-actors is an added stimulus, and tickets make it a real "show."

While children create their play, the teacher is definitely in the background. This does not mean that she is unaware of what is happening. She is constantly alert to all the play activities that are occurring, even though she is not actively directing them. By her choice and arrangement of play materials, she influences the range and quality of play. She also permits children to make their own selections of play materials, and encourages them to make their own discoveries. She does not provide models to be copied, nor does she issue too many directions. She shares the delights of children who have mastered a problem or made a discovery. She sets appropriate limits which prevent misuse of materials and safeguard the users. She enjoys children's play without entering into it. She does not play *with* the children or assume dramatic roles in their play. She remains the teacher.

Children may try to entice teachers into their dramatic play by assigning them roles, "You be the mommy, Miss B." The teacher is often tempted to accept the invitation, but she needs to maintain her role as teacher. "I'm sorry, I can't be the mommy, but I'll help you find someone. Have you asked Kate?"

The main reason that the teacher should resist becoming involved in the dramatic play is that when she becomes an active participant, she loses her identity as teacher which children need her to maintain. Also, it is not always easy to shift back into the teacher role. The teacher who is engaged in playing a dramatic role is automatically out of touch with the rest of the group. She cannot be alert to the needs of all the other children who are building with blocks, or painting, or claying, or working at puzzles.

The teacher of young children knows that play is the medium by which they learn about themselves, about other selves, and about their world. She sees vigorous, resourceful play as evidence of mental health, as a good foundation for zestful, meaningful living. She knows that play builds bodies by putting muscles to work. It also builds minds, for a child at play becomes inventive and a solver of problems. Play builds social awareness, sharpens a child's self-awareness, and allows him to give expression to some of the turbulent feelings of these early years.

We cannot afford to be casual about this major experience that we offer children. It can be purposeful or aimless, enriching or limited, but all of it will be meaningful. If we are good observers of play, we can learn about children's interests, concerns, confusions, and needs. Play is the medium through which young children learn, and through which we learn about them. Play is indeed the most "beautiful central fact of childhood."

A Place to Learn

The insistence that young people must learn more and more, faster and faster, is being felt throughout the entire school system. It is not surprising that this emphasis has reached into the nursery school, the officially recognized beginning of organized education. This rush to learning has even invaded the home and preschool experiences of children under three. A book entitled *You Can Teach Your Baby To Read,* by Glenn Doman,[15] has challenged mothers and made them feel that they should get on the educational bandwagon and start teaching their infants before it is too late. This particular book clearly states that you can start teaching your baby to read at 18 months, or "if you are very clever" at 10 months!

Fortunately, not too many parents have been captured by this appeal. One parent of a four-year-old admitted that she had tried to teach her two-year-old to read, because she thought she was supposed to and would fail as a mother if she didn't. She described a "lesson" in which she was holding up a card with the word "mommy" which the child had presumably learned. The little girl looked at it and said, "elephant." The mother tried a few more cards without getting correct responses, and then she put them away.

"Suddenly it didn't seem to make any sense," she said. "She was just a baby. I realized she would never be two again, and she needed to have time to be two, and three, and four. There would be years of school for her. And besides, what could she read at two besides those cards? I threw them away. And do you know, there was a change in that child from that day on. She was happier and freer. She laughed more, and was busy and bouncy. I guess she liked people and pots and pans better than words."

This "confession" was reassuring to me. I wish that more parents would dare to defy such pleas to hasten the learning of their children.

Kindergarten teachers have been under pressure to "ready" their children for first grade reading and writing and math. The process of "readiness" seems strictly limited to paper and pencil demonstrations that indicate awareness of differences and similarities in shapes, sizes, and numbers, and in the ability to follow directions.

Nursery schools have also felt the pressure to "teach them something." "I don't want a 'play school' for my child," is a common comment from parents who are choosing a nursery school for their child. Fathers are often critical of the school where "all they do is play." "What did you learn in school today, George?", is a question that four-year-old George must answer. "Can't you write your name yet?", is a question to which he must answer "No," possibly adding, "Not yet." But he must also feel, "Apparently I'm not doing very well."

The trend toward stuffing children with facts and figures and symbols at an earlier and earlier age is one which the good nursery school teacher must resist without apology. She knows that her children are engaged in learning some very important things, and that some of the learning which may look like play does not come easily, nor without effort. Aware that the total experience of learning in the nursery school is the best possible preparation for the learning that follows, she knows that "readiness" is not acquired only in an official "readiness period," but through the total experiences to which the children are exposed. She also knows that she needs to be able to pass on her concept of learning at the nursery school level to student teachers and to parents, so that they will understand and value it.

We no longer need to defend the fact that the nursery years

are important ones. The experiences and feelings that are laid down in these early years basically influence subsequent growth and development. The nature and quality of these experiences and feelings need definition and description.

The Head Start programs for children from culturally deprived backgrounds have captured the interest and enthusiasm of educators. To fill in the deficiencies in experience of these children and to prepare them for the schooling that follows has challenged many teachers. But to "fill in" does not mean merely to "pour in" that which has been left out of barren and impoverished environments. It means considering the whole child, recognizing his need not merely to "catch up" but to experience in meaningful "doses" the enrichment he has missed. There will be discussion of this in greater detail in the chapter on the teaching of these disadvantaged children.

When parents of preschool children ask, "But what are they learning?", the teacher needs to have some clear answers. First of all she must help parents extend their concept of learning beyond the confines of intellectual achievement. Preschool children are engaged in active learning with their bodies and their feelings, as well as their minds.

The preschool period is a time of vigorous and exciting learning of "big" muscle coordination and control, and the nursery school provides opportunities for practice and mastery. Living in small apartments cannot provide space or equipment suitable for such learning. Children cannot be permitted to climb on the record player or jump from sofa to cabinet, even though their muscles are yearning to do so. But the nursery school provides legitimate apparatus for climbing, jumping, sliding, swinging, balancing. Teachers help children to dare to use these pieces of equipment, and to develop the skills necessary for mastery. Learning to "pump" oneself on a swing is a challenging task. To "walk" by hands while hanging from the horizontal ladder is an exciting feat; to "skin the cat" on the bar is a thrilling achievement. To learn these things requires effort and persistence on the part of the child with encouragement and support on the part of the teacher.

The teacher does not expect all children to be equally well coordinated. She will not nag the reluctant child into physical activity beyond his ability or interest, but will encourage and help him without insisting that he match the achievement of the more daring and confident members of the group.

I remember a four-year-old who was afraid to climb the steps to the top of the slide, and yet he yearned to do it. He would climb up one step and then climb down. The next day he climbed up two steps and then climbed down to the safety of the ground. The teacher stood nearby, smiling with encouragement. "Some day you will climb to the top and then you'll slide down!" And eventually he did, but not right away.

The resulting confidence and delight in the well-coordinated response of his body is not only a pleasure to the child, but an essential area of learning that is too often given only casual attention. It is not the teacher's intention to make athletes of her three- and four-year-olds, but to help them to use and trust their wonderful little bodies in ways that are gratifying.

She alerts children to dangers without frightening them, pointing out the need to "hold on" when on high places. She is clear and firm about discouraging rough pushing in places that might be dangerous, and offers a helping hand to the child who seems ready to try a new feat. But chiefly she encourages the learning and rejoices with the children in their mastery.

Other important lessons gained in the nursery school are related to acquiring the graces of social living. These, too, are hard work, and do not just happen. They are not taught by the book, but by experiences with other children who are busily engaged in learning the same lessons. The nursery school is the ideal place for such learning to take place.

We must remember that the nursery school child is not too far removed from the self-centered stage of his infancy. He has experienced his world as one that revolves around him. His needs and desires are often anticipated by the important grown-ups in his life. His demands may be met with cheerful resignation by parents and older brothers and sisters ("He's only a baby") or he may meet some frustration, and learn that his wishes are not always met with alacrity. He may begin to learn to accept this fact of life, or be distressed by it, or become more demanding.

But it is not until he begins to experience living in a group of his age-mates that he can begin to learn some of the pains and pleasures of being a member of a group. He learns about the rights of others and something about respecting them, that he has rights which others will learn to respect, that there are some things he can do better than other children. He also observes that some children can do other things better than he. He learns to share. He learns the pleasures of cooperation, of doing a job together. He learns to communicate his needs in ways that are acceptable to others. He acquires the beginnings of social graces by observing and learning how other people feel about him and his approaches to them. He begins to move away from the more primitive methods of social intercourse to more reasoned and civilized approaches. He learns to ask for what he needs instead of grabbing. He learns the effectiveness of language rather than physical attack.

He learns these things, partly just from being in a group, but chiefly through the perceptive guidance of the teacher who does not preach the virtues of living amicably in a group, but who demonstrates and interprets as she teaches. She treats all her children with the respect that she hopes they will eventually acquire for each other. She knows it doesn't happen quickly or easily. She is patient with their primitive responses, but she has faith in their ability to learn more civilized responses. She commends them when they show signs of having learned to share, to cooperate, to respect the efforts or products of others. "Good for you, Charlie! You remembered to ask Timmy for the rake, instead of grabbing it the way you used to do."

The preschool child is not only primitive in his social responses, he is likely to be primitive in the expression of his feelings. Although we tend to accept the all-out crying or angry demands of infants, we find it more difficult to accept the occasional all-over explosiveness of preschoolers. Such behavior is annoying or disturbing to us, and we tend to discourage the behavior by punishing or delivering moral lectures. "Big boys don't cry!" is a common pronouncement to a three- or four-year old who is tearfully expressing his feelings of loss or despair. "It's not nice to punch your sister. Tell her you are sorry." "I don't like you when you say naughty words."

This kind of teaching (and it *is* teaching!) does not take into account the facts that young children have strong feelings, that it's good to use these feelings (rather than to deny or repress them), and that they need help in using them. Good teaching consists in accepting the feelings and in helping children to express these feelings in ways that are socially acceptable.

The young child who is crying because he is sad, disappointed, or hurt, needs comforting, not disparagement or diversion from the source of his sorrow. The child needs to cry and have his crying accepted before he can deal with the situation which touched off the tears. "You're feeling so sad. You'll feel better when you finish crying." Children can learn from each other and acquire feelings of sympathy by being exposed to this kind of teaching.

Feelings of joy and jubilation are easier for adults to accept, as long as they don't become too intense and excitable. Again, these young children have not learned to express delight in the restrained manner of adults who may smile or laugh moderately when they are pleased. Young children will shout, squeal, shriek, hoot, and holler their delight. It is primitive but genuine, and deserves to be accepted rather than inhibited and restrained.

I once walked into a classroom of three-year-olds. A child was lying on the floor, kicking her heels, flailing her arms, rolling her head and shrieking. My first thought was, "This is a full-fledged tantrum," and I looked toward the teacher for an explanation. The teacher smiled and said, "It's joy, not rage! Debby was so happy when she heard she was going to have lunch with Cindy that she just had to burst out all over with joy."

She then went over to Debby, squatted on the floor beside her and said, "You are happy that you are going to have lunch with Cindy, aren't you?" Debby ceased her vigorous movements, grinned and said, "Yes, because I like Cindy."

"I know you do," said Miss G., "and I'm glad you are having lunch with her. But it's not lunch time yet. What would be fun for you to do *now?* How about helping to mix some new dough?"

"With Cindy?" added Debby.

"That's a good idea," and the joyfully exploding Debby got up from the floor and joined the dough-mixing project.

Teachers and parents may be puzzled and bewildered or

sometimes embarrassed by this kind of primitive display of joyous feelings. They may respond by disparaging them. "You don't need to behave that way. You're a big girl now. Get off the floor, stop squealing!" There is probably no permanent damage done to the child by this kind of response, but there are clear overtones of "this is pretty foolish behavior, and you had better get over it." Such a response definitely dims the joy and instructs the child to do the same.

Adults who are dismayed or bewildered by joyful explosions are likely to be more bothered and puzzled by angry explosions in young children. These are harder to accept and more difficult to manage. They are often very threatening to the adults who view them. It's easier to understand and share joy than to understand and accept the rage.

Children need to learn to manage and use their feelings of anger and hostility, as well as to understand the causes of these powerful feelings. They also need to be protected from dangerous expression. Again, these lessons are not learned by moralistic preaching or by harsh reprisals.

The teacher of young children needs to recognize the fact that these children have strong feelings and that they have not yet learned to channel them. She also needs to have confidence that they will be able to learn a more refined use of them, and that she can help them to do this. She does not condemn the feeling, although she may need to restrain or prohibit the action which accompanies the feeling.

"I know you are awfully angry at George, but I can't let you hurt him." "Could you *tell* Andy what you need, instead of pulling his hair"? The teacher of young children helps them to put their feelings into words instead of punches and pinches. "*Tell* Joe you don't like it when he kicks you." "*Tell* Jill it makes you angry when she knocks your building down." "You can *talk* about the things that make you mad."

Young children can be helped to express angry feelings in words rather than aggressive action, and this is a step toward mature healthy management of feelings which is the goal of all good teaching.

Children can also be helped by the teacher to understand and live with feelings of fear. Too often, well intentioned adults belittle or ridicule the child who is fear-ridden. "Don't be silly, there's no lion under the bed!" "You're a big boy now, you don't need your light on!" "There's nothing in that closet to be afraid of!"

The fact is that many young children do have fears. Some are intense night terrors; some are fastened to objects or sounds, like fire engines; some are expressed in fear of the dark or the unknown, or of animals or sudden noises or quick moving objects. Some of these fears may be directly related to the occasion or the object which seems to set it off; others may be disguises for deeper fears that the child dares not or cannot express: fear of loss of love, or injury.

In the early days of nursery school, the teacher is alerted to the behavior of a child who seems uneasy or tentative about trying new things. She does not push him, or demand that he overcome his fear. She reassures him about new experiences, prepares him for what comes next, helps him to be successful and to master situations that initially frightened him. For example, the child who seems inhibited and fearful about climbing the steps to the top of the slide and then sliding down can be helped to overcome his fear. First, the teacher may accept the reality of his fear by saying, "Sometimes it's scary to try new things. I know you are a little afraid to climb up the steps, but some day you will learn how to do it, and then you won't be afraid any more. Let's watch how Tommy does it. See how he holds onto the railing? See how his feet stay on the steps? Then his leg goes over the top, then the other one, then down he slides! When you feel like trying it, I'll help you."

She doesn't nag him into the performance before he is ready, nor does she expect immediate mastery. She knows that he needs to look long before he embarks on the venture. She encourages and supports his efforts, rejoices with him when he tackles one step up and helps him to feel confidence in his eventual success. "Good for you, Kevin! You climbed up three steps! Some day you will climb to the top. Right?"

Sometimes talking about things that are frightening to children is a help to them in learning to manage and live with their fears. In one such group discussion four-year-old Barbie announced, "You know what scares me? Faces of grown-ups when they cry." The teacher's response to Barbie was, "Yes, I can understand that would be scary. You would be worried and afraid because you wouldn't know why they were crying." Or, instead of giving her interpretation, she might have asked, "Why do they scare you"? Barbie might have been able to say why, but she might not have been able to explain it. "I don't know why, they just do."

The teacher can also help children to sort out and distinguish between reality and fantasy in fears. "Could a giant really hold me in his hand?" asked Charles whose older brother had just read him the story of Jack and the Beanstalk. "If I planted a bean would it really grow to the sky?" "Are witches really real?" asked Judy. "And could she really give me a poison apple?" The story of Snow White as well as the film brought out many expressions of fear in a group of nursery school children.

The children played out their fears in simple dramatizations; they fed poison apples to paper witches. The talked out their fears with each other and with the teacher who was able to help them and reassure them about what was real and what was pretend. The child who was taken to see the film *Bambi* was shaken by a much deeper fear. The loss of Bambi's mother in the forest fire activated an intense fear of the loss of her own mother. She developed night terrors, panicked whenever her mother left the house. This was a fear beyond the help of the nursery school teacher. The teacher knew that the movie had not caused, but had released the fear. She also knew that the fear was probably based in a faulty mother-child relationship which she could not alter. She could only encourage the mother to seek professional guidance for herself and the child.

One of the most effective ways for the teacher to help young children deal with their fears is by assuring them that fears have an end. "When I was little, I used to be afraid of dogs, but now I'm not afraid any more." Positive reconditioning, which sounds more formidable than it really is, is another device for diminishing fears in young children. The child who is fearful of animals can be helped to become less fearful or eventually unafraid by introducing him to a soft, small, slow-moving animal; first letting him look at it, watching others handling it, finally touching it, then holding it. Talking about the fear also reinforces the learning. "Remember when you used to be scared to touch the guinea pig? Now you like to hold him and feed him and play with him. You really learned about guinea pigs, didn't you, and now you are not scared of them any more."

So children in nursery school are actively involved in learning some very important lessons, lessons in mastering physical skills, in understanding and managing their feelings, and in developing skills in social relationships. Through these learnings they are discovering and building a picture of themselves. They are learning what is hard, what is easy; they are learning what they can do, how they feel, how to communicate with others, what works, what doesn't. The teacher helps them learn these things. The teacher knows it is important that they learn these things, and she communicates this sense of importance to the children, as she shares their difficulties and their delights in learning.

Young children are also engaged in lively intellectual activities, even though they may not be working at arithmetic problems on the blackboard or reading from pre-primers. They acquire numerical concepts of size, weight, sequence, quantity, through experiences in the classroom. They count children, chairs, cups, crackers; compare lengths of blocks, heights and weights of children; become acquainted with descriptive terminologies: long, short, heavy, light, thick, thin, double, half, small, large, pound, inch. They learn these concepts not by rote, but by direct first-hand experiences with objects that invite definition and description.

I once observed a group of young five-year-olds experimenting with a pan balance scale. They gathered an assortment of objects around the room to weigh and compare weights. They observed that when a large object was placed on one pan, and a small object on the other, the pan with the large object went down and the pan with the small object went up. From this they arrived at the generalization that large objects are heavier than small objects.

At this point the teacher offered them two new objects, one a large toy bale of cotton about four inches square, and a small metal cube with an edge about ½ inch long. She asked the children which they thought would go down. "The big one, the cotton one!" they shouted. But when they placed the objects on the scale, the small cube went down and the big cotton bale went up! This was surprising to the children. They looked puzzled, and Peter asked, "How come? I thought the *big* one was supposed to be heavier."

The teacher then passed the bale and the cube among the children. "Look at them," she said, "feel them, weigh them in your hands. Which one feels heavier?" The children agreed that the cube felt heavier, but they could not reconcile its small size with its greater weight. "What's different about these two things?" asked the teacher.

Eager answers tumbled out. "The cotton is white and the metal is dark," said Joel.

"Would that make one heavier or lighter than the other?" asked the teacher. There was general agreement it would not.

"The cotton is fluffy and soft, and the metal is hard," said Nick.

"I think I know," said Peter, "the metal cube is *closer to itself,* and the cotton has just air around it."

This seemed to satisfy the children, and they began hunting for objects that would fit their new discovery. The teacher was pleased that they had been able to think through and state a simple definition of density.

She used the word density only after they had arrived at the principle. "I think you're right, Peter. There's a word for that 'closer to itself' quality of the metal cube: it is 'density.' Try these," and she offered a big feather and a small wooden dowel. "Same thing! The little stick is heavier; it has more density!" said Peter.

Young children learn more vividly from first-hand experiences than they do from second-hand reports or pictures. A trip to a farm teaches more about animals and farm processes than books or pictures and discussion can ever provide. A city kindergarten child who was visiting a farm dictated a letter to her teacher. She wrote, "Dear Miss Porter: A cow is bigger than a book. I thought you would like to know. Love, Allison."

A group of city-bred preschoolers were visiting a farm near their summer school. They were astonished to see that the cows ate hay instead of cereal. They asked the farmer if cows brushed

their teeth. They asked why the cows in the barn had "gates" around their necks. They learned about milking machines and pasteurizing. When they returned to the nursery school they built a dairy farm based on their observations, and later dictated a group story about Daisy, the Dairy Queen, which was full of dairy facts and vivid sensory impressions.

Schools that do not have access to farms can take trips to places of local interest that will inform and clarify: trips to railway stations, even a short trip on a train, trips to construction sites to watch the diggers and dippers, a trip to the grocery store to purchase supplies for a cooking project, or to the docks, or to a gas station.

The youngest preschool children do not need to go far afield for their first-hand learning: a trip through the building, to the basement, to the kitchen provide opportunities to acquire orientation in their immediate environment.

Older preschoolers can begin to make primitive maps, first with furniture, then with blocks. They learn about directions, and relative distances between places, about traffic regulations and safety, the importance of signs. They will ask the teacher to make appropriate signs to designate streets, roads, and names of buildings.

They become interested in various kinds of transportation, from bicycles to jets. Sometimes teachers assume that children have had experiences which they have not. A four-year-old was playing with an assortment of miniature cars and trucks in my office. He picked up the bus. I asked if he had ever had a ride in a bus. He answered, "No, but I've been on a jet," and he had!

The mother who drags her child on a whirlwind rush through the supermarket is usually and understandably focussed on completing her marketing and keeping the child in the cart, out of the range of trouble. But the teacher can conduct a modest trip to a fruit and vegetable store with a group of children, and can make it a learning situation for them. They can examine the fruits and vegetables, touch them, smell them, compare them, identify them and eventually buy some.

These purchases can then be carried back to school and studied further. The vegetables may be peeled and chopped, tasted, and cooked into soup. The fruit may be peeled and chopped or put through a grinder to make a salad or a relish. And, of course, it can be eaten! "We had soup for juice," Beth announced to her mother, "and we made it!"

Simple milk puddings, jello, muffins, cookies, even bread can be made by the children under the direction of teachers who see these cooking experiences as learning experiences. The children learn the characteristics of these various food products. They learn about quantities, how much of what is needed. They learn simple measurements: a spoonful, one-half cup, a pinch. They learn about cooking time: ten minutes or an hour, and the changes produced by cooking or baking. They learn about mixing, and the things that don't mix. They learn from the mistakes they make: too much salt, not enough liquid. They learn about degrees of heat required for various kinds of cooking, about boiling and simmering and baking. They learn the proper cookery terms through the direct experience of cooking under the guidance of the teacher who both enjoys the experience and alerts the children to its learning possibilities.

Good books are important in stimulating the intellectual interests of young children. They can learn more about turtles from live turtles than from books about turtles. But having had the direct first-hand experience of watching, handling, studying a real turtle, their knowledge of turtles may be extended by books and pictures about them. Even young children can learn that books are sources of information. When a child asks a question about an insect or a butterfly, the teacher can say, "I'm not sure what he is called, but maybe we can find out in our insect book. Let's look."

Teachers can also provide opportunities for children to look at and discuss pictures that interest them: pictures of steam shovels, trucks, boats, airplanes, fire trucks, or space ships. Children can point out the details of the picture, the parts they understand, or the confusions they have. The teacher helps them by identifying the parts about which they seem uncertain, and by clarifying their confusions.

Discussions of shared experiences, of trips or current events of common interest, stimulate the development of the children's language, increase their vocabulary, and develop skill in self-expression. This is in contrast to more rigid and limited "show and tell" periods, when children are permitted to describe an object brought from home. Unless properly directed and channeled, these can often be sterile little performances in which little learning takes place.

Children enjoy playing word games as they become aware of word sounds. Thinking of words with similar initial sounds is one of these. A teacher started the game with, "I'm thinking of a boy's name that begins with the sound of sssss." "You mean S," said Bill. "Yes," answered the teacher, "and S has the sound of sssss." Or "I see something in this room that has the beginning sound of 'ch.'"

Rhyming is also fun and challenging. "I'm thinking of a color that rhymes with 'mink,' with 'think,' with 'drink'!" "I'm thinking of a color that rhymes with 'fellow'; what is it?"

The teacher can also stimulate interest in words by labeling children's pictures and other products with their names. She encourages children to dictate stories to her. "If you would like to tell about your trip to your daddy's office, I'll be glad to write it for you." Or "You could make a book about your snowman. I'll write the words you tell me."

The teacher may give some order to the telling by asking, "How do you want to begin the story?" or "What was the first thing that happened? And what happened next?" "What would be a good way to end the story?"

The teacher of young children knows that most of these children avidly seek information. They are interested in processes: how things are made, where they come from, how they work. They search for meanings, seek definitions, understanding. "How come?" is a frequent question among preschoolers.

They are also bombarded with stimuli that teach but may also confuse. Much television viewing is a source of confusion, just as some of it has educational value. The teacher in her classroom is in a position to help children sort out and clarify their confusions. She can also stimulate them to think clearly, to ask questions, to seek answers and to find enjoyment and excitement in learning.

I believe that a good nursery school is truly an educational institution. I remember my amusement years ago when four-year-old John, who had created a strange and wonderful shape out of clay, held it up and announced, "No one knows what this is, but me. I'm the only one in the world who knows what this is." I smiled and said, "How come that you know, John?" He grinned and answered, "Education!" Apparently John felt that that was what had been going on in his nursery school.

Learning to Teach

The story of how Miss Bates (the heroine of Chapter One) became a nursery school teacher is typical of many natural born teachers who discover their role gradually through experience and training. There is no set pattern, no single program. The basic prerequisite is a genuine interest in children.

Miss Bates had always enjoyed young children. Even as a young girl, she had had a knack with them. She remembered an incident in the eighth grade when her teacher had selected her to display and describe a large picture chart of a cello to the kindergarten class. She tried to find out all she could about the instrument. She wished she had a real cello to show them. She remembered the glow of satisfaction she had felt as she taught the group about the cello. She remembered the attentive, responsive faces of the children. At thirteen she liked the feeling of being a teacher.

Miss Bates, like most of us, had memories of her own teachers: the shining ones, the grim ones. There was the kindergarten teacher who always selected the child who "sat up the straightest" to pass the scissors, but often she noticed that the chosen one was not the straightest sitter. "Teacher's pet" was something she observed in operation long before she knew the term, and she knew she didn't like it.

She remembered a fifth grade substitute teacher, probably

eager to impress the class with her authority, screaming at her because she had dropped her pencil, and sending her to the cloakroom. Then there was Miss McFee who taught seventh grade math as if she disliked the subject as well as her pupils. For a whole year she dreaded that math period and the tyranny of that teacher.

But she also remembered Miss Ellison who filled geography with people as well as with rivers and mountains and capitals; she was the teacher who provided hot cocoa for the children who had walked long distances to school through snow and icy winds. She remembered the high school teacher who taught English literature, and the England in which the literature was written. Twenty years later Miss Bates felt at home in London just because this teacher had made London's streets and bridges so vivid.

Miss Bates had sharp memories of her college teachers. There were those who were cool but competent dispensers of subject matter. There were those who imbued their lectures and their students with enthusiasm beyond the boundaries of the topic under discussion. There were those who made the library not merely a place to find answers or to complete assignments, but a place for literary prowling and discovery. She remembered two professors of Shakespeare: one who assigned 50 lines to be memorized, checked to see if she had learned them, and never knew or seemed to care that she forgot them as soon as they were written; another who made her feel that remembering certain beautiful lines would be a source of comfort and joy to her. She memorized them, savored their beauty and wisdom, and years later found that she still remembered many of the passages that had had special meaning to her.

Miss Bates attended a liberal arts college. Her major was English, not Education. In fact she took only one course in the field of education: history of education, in which she was introduced to the names and theories of historical educators from Pestalozzi to Dewey. The material was so lifeless, it seemed to have no relation to teaching or learning. It only convinced Miss Bates that she would not be interested in teaching anybody anything!

During the final lecture of the course something happened.

A visiting lecturer who taught in a small progressive elementary school in New York City described her school. Her description of the various class curricula was as lively and exciting as the preceding lectures had been dull and dry. She told how in this school, the individual classes were focussed on work study programs that also performed a service for the school. For example, the fourth grade conducted the post office. They sold stamps, mailed packages, distributed the school mail. These services required skills in math and reading. Social studies and history provided a historical background of early postal practices from the pony express to modern mechanical canceling machines. The class built a musical drama around enactments of historical events related to mail. They took trips to local post offices, and discussed them. It became important to improve handwriting, and to learn about the various kinds of letters that needed to be written, from personal notes to business letters.

Another class ran the school supply store, and the same kind of opportunities for learning by doing were provided. They learned about ordering materials, as well as selling, making change, and bookkeeping. The eighth grade ran the school print shop. They printed all school notices, and studied the history of the printed word.

Miss Bates was so excited by what she heard that she decided she must see this school in action during her next vacation. She found it just as lively and just as exciting as it had been described. Even the youngest preschool children were working and learning in their play with blocks and art materials.

The five-year-olds had built a city with blocks. The city was New York, which they were learning about from trips and discussions. "Did you know Manhattan is an island?" one of the children asked her. "That's why we have to build all these bridges." The walls were hung with vivid paintings, mostly designs.

Before she left she had convinced the school's director of her interest in learning more about this kind of education. The director asked her if she would be interested in working as an apprentice teacher with one of the younger groups after her graduation. Miss Bates was delighted at the prospect. She returned to college determined to find some children with whom she could work. A settlement house needed a story-teller, and she volunteered to take the job.

She still remembers the faces of the five- and six-year-old children in that first circle, waiting for the magic moment when the story would begin. She read them fairy stories and folk tales. She held her audience with her dramatic reading. Years later, as she looked back on the experience, she realized that she had been the star performer, and the children were the spellbound audience. This was a mistake, she later discovered. Young children learn more by being included as participants. She wanted more contacts with young children, and she wanted to learn how to become a good teacher. She could hardly wait for graduation and for the next year to begin.

Finally it came. She was assigned to the "fours" as an apprentice teacher. She discovered that this consisted of acting as an assistant to the group teacher who was a gifted, creative person. She also participated in staff conferences and meetings on curriculum practices. She had regular conferences with her "master teacher" to discuss individual children, curriculum planning, classroom procedures, teaching methods and practices. She took some courses in children's language and preschool curriculum planning, but she learned the most just by being associated day after day with good classroom teaching. She watched and listened to her teacher. At first she imitated her actions and her words. Gradually she dared to be herself. She made mistakes, and she learned from them.

Years later, after Miss Bates had acquired a degree in the field of Early Childhood Education, she looked back on her apprenticeship year as one of her richest learning experiences. It was during that year that she began to feel like a teacher, and began to assemble a pattern of some of the essential characteristics of the effective teacher of young children. She became aware of the subtleties of such teaching, as well as its challenges. She realized it was more difficult to measure the success of this kind of teaching than that of the teaching of subject matter. Even first grade teachers could measure the reading level of their children at the end of the school year. It was a little harder to assess the gains of preschool children.

Preschool teaching seemed more supporting than instructing or informing. It had a "nurturing" quality. Miss Bates discovered that the teacher needed to be aware of and alert to physical hazards that might endanger the children. There were times when she needed to provide comfort and reassurance: to offer the friendly shelter of a lap, or a helping hand with pesky buttons or stuck zippers. She recalled Marcy's comment, "I can unbutton, but not button yet." She learned that there were times when young children needed mothering, and she provided it; at the same time she did not confuse mothering with teaching.

She became aware of the power of teaching values by demonstration rather than by lecturing, moralizing, or threatening. She knew that she was teaching courtesy by being courteous to her pupils, and by approving their spontaneously gracious acts. She found herself stressing good feelings rather than labels, and she found that children seemed to understand and learn from this kind of teaching.

She learned to see her role not as a "show and tell" type of teacher, but rather as a viewer of children, a catcher of their signals, and a perceptive responder to these signals. She realized that the "wallpaper" role of standing back and permitting the child to develop was not good teaching. She recognized the difference between passive viewing and active observing. She knew that her awareness of children's needs would cue her to action when necessary.

It took time to learn that her interest in understanding children's behavior did not mean she should be tempted to become a deep-level interpreter of the behavior. She learned to describe behavior without attaching deep significance to it. She recognized behavior that was disturbing to her or to the group as troublesome to the child himself. She sought causes to the extent that she was able. She also learned to seek other professional help in understanding and dealing with behavior that was beyond her ability to understand or cope with.

She was clear that she should not assume the role of moral instructor. She recalled the moralizing of some of her own early teachers, and its ineffectiveness. "You musn't say those naughty words." "I don't like you when you behave like that." She felt strongly that young children should not be labeled good or bad. She was equally clear that certain kinds of behavior deserved approval and others needed disapproval. She began to learn the relative ineffectiveness of preaching or punishing, and the effectiveness of firmness and clarity.

Jessie Stanton, who was closely associated with the original Bank Street Schools, once wrote a humorous description of the training which should be required of every student who anticipates teaching young children. "She should have a fair education," she wrote. "By this I mean she should have a doctor's degree in psychology and medicine. Sociology as a background is advisable. She should be an experienced carpenter, mason, mechanic, plumber, and a thoroughly trained musician and poet. At least five years practical experience in each of these branches is essential." There were additional suggestions about desirable areas of training for this pluperfect paragon of a teacher, ending with the statement: "Now, at 83, she is ready!"

I think it may be possible to learn to become a good teacher of young children before the age of 83! I think Miss Bates did! But we must remember that it was the *kind of person* that Miss Bates was, combined with what she had learned, that helped her to become a good teacher of young children.

Personal Qualifications

The effective teacher of young children needs more than a body of knowledge, more than techniques and skills. Along with "knowing," she needs to have the kind of awareness of children's needs and natures that is not always found in textbooks. She needs to "tune in" on these needs, and to respond to them.

She needs to like children, to enjoy them as people, not only as amusing little entertainers. I am always a little leery of the young teacher who says that she "loves little children," as if this alone proved that she had the stuff that teachers are made of. Young children are often appealing and amusing, but they are more than "cute"; they are real.

Children do need to be loved and enjoyed by their teachers. But they need equally to be valued and accepted for themselves. The teacher who has natural warmth and affection will feel at home with all children, and they will feel at home with her.

The teacher who is hearty and affectionate is not sentimental and sweetly tolerant. She lets children know that she enjoys them; she tells them that she is glad to see them when they arrive in the morning, because she is glad. She tells them that she misses them when they are absent, because she does miss them. She rejoices in their delights and successes, she shares their pleasures, she laughs *with* them not *at* them. She smiles across the room to the child who has caught her eye and seems to need a friendly glance of approval.

The effective teacher is also able, however, to express her disapproval of undesirable behavior. She can say to a child and mean it: "I really don't like it when you spit on me. It makes me very angry." Or, "It makes me feel sad when you hurt the guinea pig. I really don't like that. How can I help you so you won't do it any more?" She knows that these comments may not bring a prompt end to spitting, or hurting the guinea pig, but they honestly convey to the child the teacher's own feelings: not rage, not condemnation, but justifiable concern and disapproval.

I have observed the acute discomfort of some student teachers when confronted with the direct honesty of preschool children. They try to disguise their embarrassment. They distract the children by dramatic stunts or entertainment. They do tricks, or they stimulate the children to wild excitement, or they become deeply involved in dramatic play from which they cannot later extricate themselves, all because they are not comfortable, not at ease with a child's frankness. I recall observing in a classroom when a somewhat overweight student teacher joined the group for the first time. John stared at her and asked, "Why are you so fat?" He was not really asking for information, nor did he intend to hurt her feelings. He was merely stating his observation in crude four-year-old terms.

Nancy, the student teacher, was startled and tried to cover her embarrassment by clowning. "I'm really made of balloons," she announced, "and if you blow me up, I'll get bigger and bigger!"

"And then will you pop?" asked John.

"Then I'll be a Zeppelin, and float away," she answered.

"Hey, come on Mike, let's blow her up!" called John. The children surrounded her, blowing and puffing and yelling,

"Blow her up, blow her up!"

It was pandemonium, and Nancy stood helpless until rescued by the teacher who said to the children:

"Nancy was really fooling you. She's not made of balloons. You know she's not made of balloons. She's made of bones and muscles and skin and nerves, just like all of us. She is just bigger than we are. She weighs more pounds, right, Nancy?"

Nancy grinned in agreement and relief.

This episode was followed by a weighing and height-measuring project that was enlightening to everyone. The teacher managed to speak to John about his comment to Nancy. "You know, John, it is not such a good idea to say things like that to people. They don't like to hear those things. It makes them feel uncomfortable. I'll try to help you remember."

Part of feeling comfortable involves the total acceptance of children as they are, without blame, without judgment. It is easy and even pleasant to accept the vitality, freshness, eagerness, and enthusiasm of young children, so long as it doesn't become too exuberant. It is not so easy to accept their more primitive expressions of anger and hostility, particularly when directed toward the teacher. Understanding that these manifestations of raw emotions are natural and childlike does not necessarily mean that teachers are equipped to accept and deal with them in ways that will benefit the child.

Young teachers are often dismayed by violent expressions of anger in their children. They feel hurt, or that somehow they have failed to instill more positive attitudes. Or they blame parents for permitting children to be so freely expressive. They tend to respond by moralizing ("It's not nice" to say or do these things), or by punishment, believing this will teach the child that there are unpleasant consequences to such undesirable behavior.

Condemnation of the primitive behavior of young children was not learned in courses in child development or human relations. It has been built into the teacher's own growing up, in the attitudes in his own home, and in the extent to which his own behavior was accepted or condemned.

What young teachers need to realize is that in accepting primitive behavior in young children, they are neither condemning nor condoning it. First, they need to let children know they are not being blamed for what they do. Second, teachers themselves must have confidence that they can help young children progress to more mature modes of social behavior.

How do they do this? By accepting the hostility in children, and by pointing out to the child the feelings he arouses in others. "I know how you feel" has become a standard teacher comment to a child who is in a state of rage through disappointment or frustration. "But I can't let you hurt Jess," or "Bill doesn't like it when you knock him down. It makes him angry. It makes him feel like hitting you." "Laura doesn't like to be pinched; *tell* her what you want." Such comments lead the child to feel that you are not condemning him, that you want to help him.

It is probably easier for a teacher to accept and deal with the hostile behavior of a child against other children, than against herself. There always seem to be some children in a group who need to challenge adult authority, to test its limits. Sometimes these challenges are disguised in dramatic overtones, "I'm going to put you in jail." Sometimes they are direct and undisguised: "I hate you. You're a stinky teacher, I'm going to cut you up and put you in the garbage can, and I mean it!"

To the young and inexperienced teacher, these threats are painful and baffling. She doesn't know what to say and she doesn't know what to do. The experienced teacher will recognize these verbal attacks not as insults to her, but as signs of anger which need interpretation. She may say, "You seem to be very angry with me, Billy. Something must be bothering you. Could you tell me? I'd like to help you, because I like you!" This is more than "turning the other cheek." It is an affirmation of her confidence that she can help him, that she does not return his anger with anger, and that she discounts the literal interpretation of his threat. She does not accuse him of being a naughty boy for saying such "unkind" things to her, nor punish him to discourage repetition.

Even more threatening are the direct attacks: hitting and kicking. The "accepting" teacher accepts the fact that the child is still in a stage of primitive expressiveness of strong feelings. She also accepts the clearly visible fact that he is enraged by something she has done or not done, and that he is directing his rage toward her. She does not need to accept the punch or the kick, and the child needs to know it. "I know you are angry at me, because I wouldn't let you hit Joe with the shovel, but you may not hit (or kick) me. I really don't like that."

A child in a major rage may need actual physical restraint by holding his hand to prevent further hitting. He surely needs an opportunity to cool off, if possible away from other children. Subsequent acceptance and return to the group will remind him that you are going to try to help him so he won't get into such troubles again. He must feel that you are his ally, not his enemy, and even though you stop him from doing dangerous things to others or to himself or to you, you still like him and believe in him, and in his ability to learn better ways of handling his angry feelings.

The effective teacher of young children needs to be the kind of person who is able to understand the appropriateness of some of the less civilized impulses of young children. She will not condemn the child for having them, or seek to overwhelm him with guilt, nor expect him to exchange them for more civilized modes of behavior just to please her. But she will also need to be the kind of person who possesses the decisiveness and clarity that safeguard children from injury to themselves or others. "Hammers are for hammering nails into wood, not for hammering people." "Blocks are to build with, not for hitting people." "Sand is for digging, not for throwing." Simple, clear, understandable rules that will be enforced are essential for peaceful, productive classroom living. And enforcement does not imply vindictive punitive reprisals. It may involve curtailment of use of materials. "I can't let you use the hammer, when you use it to hurt people. When you feel sure you can use it for hammering nails, then you may use it again." Or when, on a walk on the rocks, the "pusher" can't resist pushing, he needs to have it demonstrated that he will not be permitted to join the walkers on the rocks until he is sure he will not push them.

The enforcement of such rules frees children rather than inhibits them. Such clarity and decisiveness about what is allowed or not allowed is a positive comfort to children. They accept it without a residue of resentment. They recognize that the teacher is trying to help them.

The teacher who possesses these gifts of clarity and decisiveness (not usually learned from text books) is able to be an impartial interpreter of consequences, without condemning the offender. Her goal is to clarify the offense, its nature and hazards, to point out its consequences and enforce them, but without malice. She is the enforcer of necessary boundaries and limits, but without blame to the transgressors of these limits. She is consistently firm and unwavering, but willing and able to recognize her mistakes. This does not weaken her in the eyes of her children, but makes her seem more human. "I wasn't much help to Bobby when he started knocking down the block buildings. I wonder how we could really help him? Do you have any ideas?"

Most important of all is the teacher's relative satisfaction with herself as a person who has an ability to communicate with others, and a willingness to share her understanding and whatever skills and gifts she has.

She is aware of her own shortcomings and areas of conflict, but she is not overwhelmed by them. She is not disturbed by behavior which echoes her own problems.

She needs to be a gracious and easy giver of herself. She needs to listen to the child who has a tale to tell. She needs to share the joys and delights and discoveries of her children, as well as their disappointments and uneasy feelings of failure and frustration.

She recognizes that not all children need the same thing from her. She accepts and welcomes the unique and special individuality of each child. She will be alert to and respectful of individual differences among her children. She will not expect the child who is like a miniature hurricane to enter the room or approach his play with the quiet serene composure of a child less highly geared. She will try to help the hurricane child to use his forceful energy in ways that satisfy him but do not disrupt the more gentle zephyrs. But she will not blame nor even tame the hurricane; she will rather endeavor to direct and steer it into positive channels.

She may wish that the timid child could dare to be more assertive, or that the overly aggressive child could become somewhat more passive, but she will never set out to shape all her children into a common mold. She expects them to be different, she accepts and welcomes their differences, and helps them to do the same.

Another quality which teachers of young children need to possess or acquire is alertness, awareness, and response to the freshness and sense of wonder that these young children have.

This sense of wonder is a precious quality which somehow disappears or gets lost in a world focussed on the demands for accuracy and correctness. We are taught to define rather than describe, and very early we begin teaching young children to do the same. It's a kind of "no nonsense" approach to education, and however well intended, it usually produces a sterility and uniformity of response that closes the door to the magic of everyday experiences. Teachers of young children are in a strategic position either to encourage or stifle this awareness of wonder.

Rachel Carson in her book *Sense of Wonder*[12] describes the many simple ways in which children can be guided to experience the magic of everyday wonders. She writes, "A child's world is fresh and new and beautiful, full of wonder and excitement. It is our misfortune that for most of us, that clear-eyed vision, that true instinct for what is beautiful and awe-inspiring is dimmed and even lost before we reach adulthood." She gives us a recipe for encouraging and sustaining the sense of wonder. She describes taking a young child into the woods on an "expedition of exciting discovery" not just to teach the names of plants and insects. She also reports how much the child learned and remembered, not through drill, but through the delight of a shared experience.

A group of five-year-olds on a walk in the woods found a worm. They stopped to look at it, getting down on their knees to worm level. The teacher asked if a worm could walk. Jeff, who had been studying the slow motion of the worm, replied, "Yes, a worm has a way of walking. He wiggles into himself, then stretches out and flats himself along in a jiggering kind of way. I think his head goes first."

To me this is a piece of pure descriptive poetry, with rich wormy images. Jeff had the freshness of viewing, uninhibited by the need to produce a correct answer. He also had a teacher who encouraged the expression of "direct" sensory impressions. She followed this worm-walking observation and description with opportunities for viewing and describing the "walks" of other creatures, insects and animals. It was observed that "grasshoppers bounce like rubbery bands, snip, snap, bounce!" "Turtles walk like little old men, with a shell house on their backs."

"The praying mantis is saying his prayers. His knees are jointy and bent, and he waves his praying hands." "Snails smear a slow trail." Could anything be slower than that?

This teacher was herself alert to the wonders of nature, and stimulated the children to look, listen, touch, as well as to describe their observations and sensations. "What does it look like? How does it feel? Watch how it moves." She sharpened their senses and they responded with increasing awareness.

This kind of teacher hears and responds to children's spontaneous expressions of delight. As Timmy dreamily slides his fingers through finger paint, she asks, "What does it feel like Timmy?" Timmy answers, "It feels like pudding, smooth with no raisins, and no spoon!" Then, as his fingers swept in free circular motions, he grinned and said, "But now it's a bicycle, and the wheels are turning and slipping in sloop."

Four-year-old Alice remarks as she pats and pokes and smooths her clay, "Clay is quiet, quiet as fingers in clay, quiet as a cushion and squeezy." The teacher had not asked for a definition of clay, but she caught Alice's description and smiled in agreement.

Children were recalling a trip to the farm. They remembered not just what they had seen, but what they smelled and what they touched. "Remember the cow?"

"Yes, she was fat and full of milk in the underneath part. It had handles for the farmer to squeeze out the milk and the milk went squirting into the pail."

"She breathed warm on my hand. Her eyes were like wet lollipops and she looked at me with her lollipop eyes."

"She licked my hand. Her tongue was warm and prickly with sandpaper suds."

This is good reporting. If the teacher's response to these vivid recollections of sensory experiences is enthusiastic and appreciative, children will continue to seek and find imaginative ways of expressing their thoughts. They will use language as a creative tool, not merely for factual reporting of events, but for vivid and often poetic descriptions of experiences and observations. They will become sharper observers, and clearer reporters.

The teacher provides the opportunities for discovery; she also alerts children to the sensory potentials of all experiences

through asking questions—"What does it feel like, how did it sound?, etc." And she shares the children's delight in their free imaginative expression.

The effective teacher is full of ideas without imposing them on her children; ideas for ingenious use of materials, as well as ideas for resolving competitive situations involving "whose turn it is to use the new dump truck."

This does not mean that she can solve all problems, or that she never makes mistakes. In fact, she gains stature in her group by being able to admit that she has made a mistake. "That wasn't such a good idea I had for fixing the guinea pig's cage. It didn't work. We'll have to find a better way." Or, "I thought I knew how to help you in your mixup, but I guess I was mixed up myself!" It is comforting to children to know that even teachers can make mistakes, can admit it, and try to remedy it.

Our effective teacher has compassion for the troubled and the troublesome child, realizing that he is often troublesome because he is troubled. She tries to find reasons for it. She talks with the child's parents to discover possible causes for the be- havior. Is there a new baby in the household who seems to be consuming the attention of the parents? Has there been serious illness or a death in the family? Have parents been away from home? Are there anxiety-provoking prospects of change in the family atmosphere: anticipation of moving to another town, change of job? Discovering causes of disturbing behavior is the first step toward helping the child to deal with it. Sometimes more expert help is required to find these causes, such as the counsel of a guidance clinic or a psychiatric consultation and evaluation.

The teacher should be able to recognize and accept the nor- mal range of behavior that may be disruptive to group har- mony or bothersome to her or to the child himself. She expects to find a certain amount of explosive behavior in every group, and she endeavors to direct this aggressiveness into constructive channels. Work bench projects, sawing and hammering can re- lease aggressive needs with gratifying results. A child can pound out his anger and produce a truck with wheels that really turn!

But there are children whose need for hostile aggression is so intense that they cannot be steered in the direction of more positive expression and release. These children are usually very disruptive to the peace of the group. They are often impulsive, quick to attack or destroy. They find little satisfaction in the materials and activities of the nursery school classroom. Their relationships with other children are fleeting or violently possessive or indiscriminately hostile. These are usually deeply fearful children, with a very low sense of self-value. This is the kind of child that even the most experienced and understanding teacher cannot always succeed in helping, without psychiatric guidance and direction. Sometimes it is not wise to continue to keep such a child in the group. This is not meant to condone the casual expelling of a child whose demands and needs are greater than a teacher can meet, and whose behavior causes major disruption to the rest of the group. It should be done only when no alternative plan can be made which will be beneficial to the child and to the group.

This effective teacher is not a paragon of all virtues. She is very human. She gets discouraged and annoyed, sometimes with children, sometimes with parents, sometimes with the director or the janitor, and sometimes with herself. But she never really loses her determination to guide her children to become confident learners, eager and trusting.

She needs to be physically strong and able. Nursery school teaching is not for the frail and disabled. It requires strength and stamina including good knee joints; there's a lot of getting down to the child's level which is often on the floor. Along with getting *down,* there needs to be agility in getting *up* when it is necessary to speed across the room to prevent an impending major disaster.

She needs to be able to pick up a child who needs picking up, as well as to pick up hollow blocks and boards and heavy equipment that needs moving. Her sitting-down moments are rare. This does not mean that she is constantly in motion or hovering tensely. However, she is constantly aware and alert as to what is happening in every part of the room, or the playground. She is quick in getting to the area where she is needed. Her visual range is wide, and her muscular response is speedy. She is swift without swooping. She must be healthy, strong, and agile. It is hard to visualize a slow-motion teacher of young children. Her pace is not frantic, but steady. She moves swiftly when speed is indicated. She doesn't wait until Ben's block has crashed on Michael's skull before intervening. If possible, she gets to the scene and intercepts the crash, and then she deals with the situation. But first she needs to get there!

It is often surprising and dismaying to young students to find that nursery school teaching carries substantial housekeeping responsibilities. An effective teacher must be the kind of person who can not only set up and organize a room which invites learning, but can also keep it that way. And that means work.

This does not mean that the teacher spends her days in frantic tidying. It does mean that she keeps materials in good working condition. Paints are kept fresh and bright; brushes are clean and ready for use; clay is soft, not caked and dried; blocks are arranged according to size and shape; accessory materials are accessible; books are mended; puzzles are intact; broken toys are removed. The room has a shipshapeness that invites rather than repels. And the teacher is the one who produces and maintains this order.

She encourages children to share in the process of housekeeping, but she doesn't resent it or feel that it somehow diminishes her respectability as a professional person to keep her room in order. She takes pride in an attractive, well-organized room with materials in order, because she knows this favors learning.

The teacher who expresses delight in doing and learning will, of course, be more successful in her teaching than the ever solemn, serious one. Not that the nursery school teacher finds delight in every moment, or wears a perpetual smile; but she comes to her job of teaching expecting to enjoy it. She brings cheer to her classroom, and often finds even more there to cheer her than she brought.

Morning greeting time is important. It can set the tone for the day. Peter, the obstreperous one, came bounding into the room, beaming. Miss A. smiled at him and said, "Good morning, Peter. You look so cheery today."
Peter: "Yup, that's because I feel hap-hap-happy!"
Miss A: "I'm glad." Then she remembered the previous day

which had not been such a "hap-hap-happy" day for Peter. Without attempting to cast gloom on his present cheery state, she recalled his mood of yesterday.

"Remember yesterday, Peter?"

Peter: "Yup, mad, mad, mad!"

Miss A: "You certainly were grumpy."

Peter: "Do you ever be mad and grumpy?"

Miss A: "Oh, yes, sometimes I feel mad and grumpy. I guess everyone does."

Peter: "Why do you be mad?"

Miss A: "When I have to do things I don't want to do, or when I get too tired, sometimes I feel grumpy."

Peter: "But today you feel cheerp, cheerp, cheery, just like me, right?"

Miss A: "Right! Just like you!"

It was a cheery beginning for both Peter and his teacher, and somehow it set the tone for the whole day.

Organizing
Space and Materials

What a teacher *does* in a classroom is influenced partly by what she *knows* or has learned, and partly by the kind of person she *is*. The kinds of insights and values or qualities that have been built into her as a person before she became a teacher usually influence what she does in her classroom.

In her "doing," the teacher of young children is first confronted with *space* in which to "do the doing." Her first responsibility in preparing the kind of program that will engage the interests and minds of the children is to arrange the space and to organize the materials in it in ways that will challenge and capture interest.

Few nursery schools have been planned, designed, and built to be nursery schools. And some of those that have been designed were planned and built by people who had no real understanding of the educational needs of young children. Lilliputian toilets and wash stands, low hand rails on stairwells, large barren rooms with a set of low tables and chairs seemed to satisfy their sense of adequate space for preschoolers.

At least one such building on the campus of a great college includes leaded glass windows which open outwards and can be easily reached from window seats which invite climbing to investigate the window-opening mechanism. The fact that this is a second-floor classroom adds another danger factor that the planners neglected to consider.

But most teachers are confronted with inherited rather than deliberately built-in challenges in adapting space that was never intended for use by young children. Church basements, lodge halls, old houses have all been tackled by ingenious teachers who have managed to.convert them to useable space for play and learning.

Again, such adaptation is not something that is always taught to the young teacher. But her understanding of children's needs and interests, plus her sense of order and organization of space for use, aid her in the job of adaptation.

. First, she scans the total space available, and begins to visualize the kind of organization for use that will be most desirable. She estimates the potential traffic lanes, the incoming and outgoing areas. She spots the likeliest free open spaces needed for blockbuilding. She is aware of light sources for table activities and painting and books. In her mind, she begins to place suitable shelving near the appropriate activities: block and accessory shelves near the block area; shelves for puzzles, crayons, paper, collage materials, manipulative toys near the tables; book shelves near the library area. She selects a compact housekeeping corner or area separate from the other activity areas. She looks for display space, where science and nature exhibits may be assembled and examined. She thinks about storage; where to keep paints and clay and dough and paper; the accessibility of materials which children themselves can manage and those which the teacher needs to dispense.

She looks around with an eye to the decorative aspects of the space. If she has a choice of wall color, she chooses a light cheery tone that illuminates the space, but does not glare. She plans a tack rail for hanging children's paintings. She may display a few colorful posters that are decorative and eye-catching, but she will not clutter her walls with sweetly saccharine pictures of children that may appeal to adults but have no particular appeal to children whose work room this will be. Pictures of animals, of transportation, boats, airplanes, trucks, are often of interest to young children, but they should not dominate the decor.

To curtain or not to curtain windows is another decision the teacher must make. If the outlook from windows is bleak and uninviting, bright curtains will probably add a note of cheerfulness and color. If the outlook is one of natural beauty, it may seem more suitable not to shut it out, but to allow it to come into the room through clear uncurtained windows. Some stiff rooms seem softened by curtains.

There are differences of opinion among teachers concerning the display of children's paintings: the number and manner in which they should be hung. Some teachers believe that every child in the group should have a painting on display. This usually means that walls are plastered with pictures, often one on top of another, serving as an automatic storage unit; that is, all of Sally's paintings are stacked on top of each other until the hooks can hold no more. The visual result is an untidy stuffed bunching of curling papers that is neither attractive nor appealing.

Other teachers feel that it is not essential that each child be represented in the display of paintings. For some children, it is extremely important, and for others it is not. The purpose of displaying the paintings should not be for reward or recognition, but for adding color and pattern to the room. Accordingly, the hanging should be carefully planned and discreetly and suitably spaced as part of the total decorative scheme.

One teacher designed simple unfinished wooden frames with poster board mats to which a child's painting could be taped. This framing device gave the paintings an official air of respect, and often brought out some of the primitive beauty that was lost in lone hanging.

Plants are another decorative feature of classrooms. Children can share in the care by watering them. However, the responsibility for plant care needs to be the teacher's. Those who lack the "green thumb" will probably be content to do without them.

The problem of clothing storage is another planning responsibility of the teacher who is engaged in organizing space. Is there room for individual "cubbies" or lockers? Should they be in the main play room, or outside of it? How about hooks, or hangers on a bar? Where to put boots and caps and scarves and mittens? How identify individual storage space, with names or pictures or symbols? These are just a few of the questions that must be considered.

An individual cubby or open locker is desirable. Each child can have his own putting-place, with hooks for hanging, a shelf for small clothing, and a place for boots and rubbers under the seat shelf. This is also a cozy place to which he can retreat when he needs to get away from the group, as well as a storage place in which to keep his take-home treasures.

If the room is large enough to contain the lockers, it is easier for teachers to supervise the dressing and undressing routines. If they cannot be accommodated in the classroom, they should be adjacent to it.

The method of identifying lockers is another planning decision that teachers must make. Possible choices are colors (over-all interior painting in various colors, or small tapes of color) or symbols (circles, squares, triangles, lines, etc.) or pictures, or names, or a combination of some of these. I favor the clearly printed name of each child, plus a small picture or symbol which he may identify before he can read his name.

One teacher gathered some discarded lotto game picture cards of animals and birds, and allowed each child to choose a picture which was then placed in his locker and labeled with his name. "This is MY locker," said four-year-old Kurt. "But I'm not really a kangaroo." Then, as he studied the picture and the name, he added, "Hey, Kurt, and kangaroo, we both begin the same! You know, with K!"

Every teacher will hope for a low sink and counter for water play as well as for washing up. She will also hope that bathroom facilities of appropriate size and number (preferably at least one toilet and basin for eight children) will be adjacent to the main playroom.

In all-day nursery programs which involve the serving of lunch followed by naps, there obviously needs to be suitable space for these activities and the equipment they require. Storage for cots and blankets adjacent to the nap space is essential. When eating and napping occur in the same room in which children play, there needs to be a careful programming of activities to prevent chaotic transition from one activity to the next. Strategic arrangement of the equipment involved can often aid in harmonious management of even complicated situations.

The doll corner needs child-size furnishings, either bought

or homemade. There should be no clutter of too much and too many. The teacher will have a reserve supply of "surprises" or new things to bring out from time to time for refreshment and stimulation. There should be both male and female dress-up clothes.

While the teacher has been organizing the space into harmonious work areas, she has also been thinking of the materials, the furnishings and the equipment that will be needed to stimulate creative play. If she is lucky, she will be able to design shelving that will be appropriate and attractive as well as functional. She will select tables and chairs that are sturdy and attractive. She will choose play materials that issue invitations to explore and discover: the "raw" materials that have been mentioned before—paints, clay, crayons, paper, paste, blocks, and the things that go with them.

I can never think of organizing and setting up a nursery school classroom without recalling an article written by Claudia Lewis of Bank Street College, called "Equipped With an Oak Tree." In it she describes setting up a classroom in a little shack in the Cumberland Mountains. It was literally "equipped with an oak tree" which provided leaves, sticks, branches, bark and acorns as potential play materials. There was also dirt and mud, and eventually a clay bank was found. There was a brook with pebbles. There were logs for bridges, and berries for paints. And, of course, there was the ingenuity of the teacher who created something out of what seemed nothing. She also enlisted the interest and support of parents. Mothers sewed scraps into dolly quilts and curtains for the school. Fathers made benches and trestle tables and simple shelves. No elaborate and tempting catalogs of equipment and materials were needed to provide a setting rich in potentials for learning and delight. What *was* needed was the imaginative mind of the teacher who was able to create something lively and lovely out of simple, natural ingredients.

In considering the needs for equipping the indoor space, I have not meant to neglect the need for planning and organizing the outdoor play space. This will vary according to the nature of the play space, of course.

The first concern of the teacher will be for suitable fencing or enclosures that will safeguard the children and keep them within her visual range. A flat paved or blacktop area for wheel-barrows and wagons is desirable, as well as an area for building with hollow blocks. Suitable climbing devices, horizontal ladders or curved arcade ladders, and ladder boxes should be placed away from slides and swings. Swings (with soft, flexible seats) should either be enclosed with low boundary fences to safeguard the unaware non-swinger, or be placed in areas of no traffic. Movable boards, saw horses, gangplanks should be available for construction. A digging hole, as well as a sandbox, is desirable. Rakes for leaves, shovels for dirt and snow, pails and sieves, scoops and tins for dirt and sand play—all are important tools for out-of-door-activity. Access to water, for water "painting" and mixing with sand and dirt, is another essential when season and weather permit.

As in planning indoor space, the teacher must organize the total space for its best use; visualizing traffic lanes, providing safeguards for the use of apparatus, spacing equipment appropriately, as well as planning suitable storage areas.

In play areas where all portable materials and equipment must be put away at the end of the day, storage can be a major problem. But even where this is not essential, places for keeping materials need to be provided. It is good to have storage sheds for wheel toys and sand toys. Plastic wash baskets for hauling sand toys to and from the sand box are helpful. Shelving for hollow blocks and boards protects them from excessive weathering. They also provide a sense of order to the space, and issue more appealing invitations for building and construction than do blocks that are scattered all over the place.

Some climates permit an indoor use of outdoor space. Picnic type tables and benches, which may be left outside, can be used for the usual table activities of using clay, dough, crayons. Easels or their equivalents may also be used out of doors. Again the teacher must exercise judgment in spacing these activities so that they will be within her visual range, and will not interfere with other more motor activities.

Part of the job of organizing space and the materials in it involves responsibility for keeping it in order and good repair. A wagon with a broken handle or a missing wheel is hardly conducive to dramatic hauling play. It should be removed until it can be repaired. Splintery boards and blocks should be removed and sanded. Rusty nails and shovels should be discarded. Junky materials can only invite junky play and further misuse. This applies to both indoor and outdoor materials, and the teacher is the one who must constantly check to see that all equipment is in good condition and workable order.

Indoor and Outdoor
Activities

The teacher, who has either had the fun of planning and setting up her classroom from scratch, or has struggled with the challenge of adapting and changing space that was poorly planned and organized (whichever was her lot), has now prepared her space. The place is furnished, decorated and equipped. Her next consideration is to plan and provide for the activities that will occur in this space.

Some of the activities will be influenced by the location of the school and the climate in which it operates. Is it rural or urban, tropical or winter-chilled? Will children need to spend most of the time indoors, or outdoors, or will it be possible to plan a partly indoor and partly outdoor program?

Let's assume that the latter choice is possible. In a nursery school which has a morning session only, the teacher plans the morning to include a variety of activities as well as a range of pace and action. The first part of the morning is often the "work period" or "free play time."

I am always a little uneasy about the "free play" label, since it implies a kind of "anything goes" free-for-all atmosphere that is not intended. The "free" part means that children are free to select the activity in which they wish to engage. They are not coerced or trapped into using materials of the teacher's choice. They are free to use them in their own individual ways.

They are not free to misuse them or to use them in ways that are disturbing to others.

The room is organized to issue invitations to a variety of activities. Paints are prepared and ready for use; blocks are always on the shelves; the doll corner is always set up; table toys, puzzle and manipulative toys are accessible. Dough or clay may be set up with suitable utensils: tongue depressors, rolling pins, cookie cutters. A table with an enticing collection of collage materials for pasting may be ready and inviting.

During this period, children are encouraged to choose the activity and materials that appeal to them. Some children will leap into the room, sure of what they want to do; others may need to wander and watch a little before becoming involved. Some children may need to be steered in the direction of an activity in which they can't quite manage the first step by themselves.

A child who seems to be longing to enter the block-building area can sometimes be helped by having the teacher place a stack of blocks near him with a casual comment; "You could use these." Or she may place a lump of dough or clay before the child who is watching, and smilingly ask, "Would you like to try it?" as she pats or pokes it herself. But she does not insist that the child produce something or become actively engaged. She knows that some children need time to watch before they can act.

During this work period, there will be a busy hum of activity that may occasionally erupt into noisy explosions. There will be groups of children block-building, painting, working at table activities, engaged in doll-corner dramatizing, or playing with water. All these activities will be going on at the same time.

To the casual viewer it may seem like bedlam, but to the trained eyes and ears of the teacher, it represents a scene of multiple learning situations in which children are lustily engaged in working out the challenges involved in each play situation.

In the block area, for example, these questions are being asked: How to balance a big block on a smaller one? How to bridge an open space? How many blocks to make a roof? How to make an elevator that will really work? The teacher is aware of the challenges, and is on hand to help the builders find solutions. She doesn't solve the problems for them. She helps them to find answers by asking questions that will stimulate their thinking. "Do you think a longer block would work?" "Have you tried *this* shape?" "What do you think it needs?" "Would a piece of cord help?"

She also helps by keeping the area clear of obstructions. She quietly puts away scattered blocks or accessory materials that are not being used. She encourages children to build away from the shelves as a safeguard to their buildings. She helps them to build away from each other to prevent accidental destruction. She definitely discourages the use of blocks as weapons or missiles. Blocks are to build with, not to throw or crash. By respecting each child's effort and construction, the teacher demonstrates that each building has value and deserves respect.

The block-builder intent on construction is not only building a part of his world by re-enacting experiences of interest to him, he is learning to control the blocks and to create new forms. He learns the relationship between the different lengths, how many squares make a unit, how many units make a double unit, how many doubles make a "quad" or a "longie" as they are often called. Actually he is learning some basic mathematical concepts of size and shape and quantity. And the teacher is helping him to sort out and understand these concepts.

What are the painters learning? First of all they are learning what happens when you put a brushful of color on paper. Does it drip? Does it stay in one place? What happens when you put another color on top? Is it the same?

Ruth Shaw, the creator of finger paint, tells a story about two children finger painting for the first time. One child had made the exciting discovery that red and blue made purple, and he was announcing it to his neighbor. "Did you know that red and blue make purple?" he called out to her with great excitement. Elizabeth admitted that she didn't. She placed some red paint on her paper and then some blue near it. But nothing happened.

"Mine is not purple," she said.

"You have to mix them!" said Mike.

"Oh," said Elizabeth, as she swished the colors together into purpleness, "you mean red and blue and ME makes purple!"

We do not believe in giving children models to copy or outlines to fill in. We give them the same freedom to discover patterns that we offer in discovery of color combinations. Some children will saturate the paper with color on top of color, some will produce wispy streaks of color, some will discover the delight of dots of color scattered over the paper, some will delight in the mastery of stripes, some will arrange masses of color adjacent to each other.

Eventually, as some mastery in handling the brush is acquired, primitive representative paintings may appear; faces, or houses, or trucks, or the sun. Often these are attempts at copying the more representative pictures of older brothers and sisters.

The role of the teacher in the painting situation is primarily that of the stage setter. She provides clean brushes, clear shining colors, and paper. She may have easels or a counter, table top, or even floor painting space. She varies the combinations of colors from sets of the primary colors plus black, to sets of pastels that she has mixed, or a set of warm yellows, reds, oranges and browns, or some subtle cerise, pink, purple, or cool green and electric aqua shades.

Having set up the situation, she retreats. She may demonstrate how to prevent a drip, to the child who is bothered by the drip and wants help in managing it. But she does not tell the child what or how to paint, and she doesn't ask him what he has painted. She may comment on the color or the design to indicate her interest. "Your painting is full of gay colors." Or "Red, red, all over your paper! You like red, don't you?" Or "Dots and drips, that looks like fun, Anthony."

Three-year-olds and sometimes fours for whom painting is a new experience may experiment with painting their hands or each other. This can be discouraged by quietly stating that paints are for paper not people, and then helping wash up.

There are those who feel that finger-painting is merely a glorified mud play. The material is more plastic and sensory than liquid paint. Some children delight in its smooth squishiness, and others seem uneasy or reluctant to try it.

Salt dough and clay offer children opportunities to get their hands into the material, to feel it, to pat and smooth it, to poke it, to roll it, to shape it. Tools for slicing and rolling (tongue depressors and wooden cylinders or rolling pins) are intriguing and fun to use. But hands are fun, too.

Again, the teacher's function and role in relation to these plastic materials is first to present them in their best state. Clay needs to be kept in moist balls, covered with damp cloths or in plastic containers to preserve its moisture. Dough must also be kept in containers that prevent drying out. Children can be helped to make their own dough mixtures. There is a kind of magic in mixing the salt and flour, then gradually adding the colored water, and finally after spoon-mixing and hand-mixing, producing a lump of dough.

Having made the dough, the teacher does not instruct the children in its use. A young four-year-old in one of his first days at school was eagerly trying all the wonderful materials that he saw. He finished painting, and spying a bowl of dough on the table, announced, "Now I'm going to do dough! Hey, how do you do dough?" The teacher did not show him "how to do dough." She smiled, gave him a lump, and said, "Feel of it, Mitchell. What do you think you could do with it? Here are some things you could use," pointing out the rollers and slicers. He patted it, rolled it flat, cut some slices, beamed and said, "Yeah, I can do dough!"

A student teacher who was sitting at a table where clay was being presented for the first time took a lump in her hands, and in a few moments had modeled a most exquisite little turtle. The children, who had been squeezing, poking, rolling, pounding their clay balls, watched the modeling, and when it was finished, they pushed their clay to the middle of the table and said, "Make one for me!" They knew that they couldn't possibly make what she had made. They lost interest in their own exploring of the nature of clay and in their confidence in being able to produce anything. This had not been the student's intention, and she learned a vivid lesson about why teachers do not present adult-made art models to young children. Such a practice shuts off initiative and daring to explore the potentialities of any material. It inhibits and frequently terminates interest. It's as if the child said "It's no use; I can't possibly make that kind of thing," because he knows he can't, and his own level of production seems worthless.

The same principles apply to crayoning or cutting and pasting or collage. The teacher provides the materials and the tools, and then she steps aside and lets the children discover their own ways of using the materials. Often these are more ingenious and imaginative than any models she might provide.

I once observed a cutting and pasting group of four-year-olds during the Hallowe'en season. Pumpkins and jack-o-lanterns were in the eyes and minds of these children, and they wanted to make some. The teacher had set out sheets of orange and black construction paper for those who wanted to be part of the project. Paste and paste brushes, scissors, black crayons and a box of assorted bits of crinkled white paper were placed on the table. "But I can't make the round," commented Bobby.

"How about a paper plate?" asked the teacher. She helped to hold the plate while the children traced around the edge in black. Each child then had a black circle on an orange sheet. But nothing remained the same from that moment on. Some children drew crude faces within the circle; some children tried cutting out the nose, eyes and mouth. One child pasted white paper under the cut-out features. One added ears; another pasted a curly white beard on her pumpkin. Betsy cut out her pumpkin in an elongated shape, ignoring the outline completely, "because mine is a skinny pumpkin." Joan cut out hers, then managed to paste it onto another paper so that it stood out in a three-dimensional way. This was tricky to do; she asked the teacher for sticky tape to help her.

The end result of this pumpkin-making session was an assortment of ingeniously contrived pumpkin faces, each unique and different, each representing its maker's individuality of conception and production. One turned out not to be a pumpkin at all. Peter studied his circle and announced, "I think I'll make a clock," and he did. He meticulously cut out two hands and fastened them to the center with a paper clip. He asked the teacher to make the numbers, "because I don't know how yet." "Is it a pumpkin clock?" asked Mark. "No," said Peter, "it's just a plain clock, only orange."

Children engaged in working with manipulative toys at the table, puzzles and assorted put-together construction sets, frequently need no instruction or demonstration. If a child gets stuck with a puzzle, the teacher may help him by pointing out similar outlines or shapes that will provide clues and encouragement. And she will share his pleasure and satisfaction in having successfully completed it. "That was a tricky one to do—but you did it!" She discourages dumping and mixing the pieces from several puzzles because this results in confusion which children cannot resolve. She suggests putting the completed puzzles in the rack or on the shelf, before tackling a new one, to avoid the confusion of clutter.

The teacher's role toward children who have chosen dramatic play in the doll corner is that of alertness to what is going on, offering a helping hand to those who may be stuck with pesky fastenings of dress-up clothes; helping the child who wants to get into the play, but doesn't know how; steering disrupting children into constructive channels; entering into the mood, but not into the action of the play itself.

If there is a sick baby, she may ask if they need a doctor and may try to recruit one. If the family is going on a train trip, she may ask if they have tickets, or who is the conductor. She asks the kind of question that carries the play to a next step of dramatic complexity; or she may suggest a piece of equipment or material that gives the play dramatic validity—real cereal to serve at the table or tools to repair the broken train wheel.

She is alert to signals that the play is becoming wild and overstimulating, and she either steps in with suggestions that alter its course or change its flavor, or she terminates it with a decisive announcement that this kind of play is too disturbing to other people or too silly or too dangerous, and it has to stop. And she means it!

If play has reached this stage of wildness and disturbance, it probably should have been stopped or steered in another direction much sooner. The teacher who arrives too late to prevent, and who has to stop, behavior that has become disruptive or wild must be able to offer some appealing suggestions that will capture the interest of the children, as well as terminate the disruptive play.

The work period is a busy active time for both children and teachers. Children are actively involved in working out solutions to the multiple challenges offered in a well-stocked classroom.

They are confronting problems in human relationships as well as in mastery of materials and mechanics. They are facing facts about themselves and their feelings in this wonderful arena of play.

The teacher is teaching every moment. She is teaching concepts of space relationship when she asks a child in the block corner a question that helps him understand the length of block he needs to roof his airport. She is teaching respect for and delight in discovering the multiple and myriad uses of all the "raw" materials with which she stocks her classroom, by the order in which she keeps them. She is teaching respect for individual needs and differences by respecting them herself. Her "program," her "curriculum" is a reflection of her educational philosophy. She teaches not by lecturing, but by sharing her enthusiasm for learning, and by responding with enthusiasm to the discoveries of her children. She is constantly alert to the multiple learning situations that are occurring in her classroom, and she is responding to them in ways that confirm and teach. A question, a smile of encouragement, or a beam of approval, a friendly warning, a clear prohibition, these are her teaching tools, and she uses all of them.

It sometimes appears as if the important teaching and learning in the nursery school occurs only in the classroom. The out-of-doors time is too often used primarily as an energy outlet period. It is a time for the racing, running, shouting that was discouraged or not permitted in the classroom. "That's an outdoor voice" announces the teacher who is trying to soften the tone of the indoor playtime.

The outdoor part of the program deserves to have a more important place in the teacher's plan. It should be more than merely a "now-you-may-be-wild" time. It can be active, but this does not mean unplanned.

The varieties of out-of-door play spaces for nursery schools are almost as great as the varieties of indoor space. In many large city nursery schools, out-of-door play time is referred to as "roof time," for the logical reason that the playground is on the roof. A roof play space sets its own limits. Obviously it must be securely fenced. It is undoubtedly hard surfaced, and, of course, it lacks dirt and grass and trees and growing things.

But except for the lack of natural "equipment," it offers a self-contained area for vigorous active play that serves the large muscles of preschoolers just as well as the garden variety of playground. There is something about climbing a real tree that cannot be equaled by a jungle gym climb. But even roofs can have climbing equipment that challenges muscles and brings satisfaction to the climber.

Many nursery schools are fortunate in having playgrounds that are spacious and natural, with dirt and grass and trees and rocks. Some even have hills and hollows, and one I know of has a brook.

But just nature is not enough, although leaves, acorns, horse chestnuts in the fall and violets, dandelions, and apple blossoms in the spring are exciting and beautiful to see and feel. Even young children can be helped to appreciate and enjoy the magic of seasonal changes, but they also need objects in the outdoor space that will challenge muscles as well as minds and senses. They need a variety of equipment that will satisfy their urge to run and climb and jump, to balance, to slide, to swing, to move through space with agility. The preschool period is one of major physical development of the large muscle system of shoulders, arms, and legs, and these develop by use.

In these days of apartment living, children are often denied opportunities for the kind of vigorous physical activity which their growing bodies demand, but which the neighbors can't accept. There is no space for running; jumping is not allowed, and climbing is restricted.

The well-equipped nursery playground provides space and equipment for all of these vigorous activities. The teacher organizes the space and the things in it for the best possible use.

A fence that bounds the space is an essential safeguard. Next, the best arrangement of the equipment must be decided. Swings are placed where there is little traffic, or if possible enclosed with a low railing that reminds wanderers that swings are swinging. Hollow building blocks, boards, and sawhorses are adjacent to a flat area where construction can go on out of traffic lanes. A digging place is planned so it will not be a menace to wheel toy activities, or to casual runners. The sand box is put in a spot away from slides and climbers. All the portable ladders, gang planks, boards and sawhorses are in an area that is suitable for setting up challenging arrangements for climbing, balancing or bouncing. Traffic rules may be needed—one way up and another way down—or simply one-way traffic regulations that make for safety.

A storage shed for keeping sand toys and assorted small toys protected from weathering and loss is a necessity. Sometimes it is possible to design a double purpose shed that serves for storage (inside) as well as a high spot for climbing and dramatic play, by utilizing its flat roof with a railing along its edge.

The ingenious teacher will always be on the lookout for odds and ends that will add a note of drama or refreshment to her playground play: lengths of hose for firemen, pumps for garage men, rubber tires for swings or rolling.

The teacher who has planned and organized her playground with the needs of her children in mind will also have a clear idea of the purpose and function of outdoor play, and the ways in which she can help to make it meaningful and satisfying.

It needs to be active, but it cannot be permitted to become too wild. Such play in contagious and overstimulating and often leads to dangerous rough-and-tumble. Some children are frightened by this kind of play at the same time they seem attracted by it.

A set of reasonable rules will help to keep play within safe bounds: no pushing from high places; no ramming into people or knocking down buildings when children are inside. It also helps to steer children in the direction of having a plan or an idea of what they will want to do when they go outside. A discussion while putting on outdoor clothing, or a song, "What shall we do when we go outdoors?" may help to channel the potential explosiveness of the high-geared child to whom out-of-doors means a booming, crashing, racing, and roaring about.

The teacher, who is teaching out-of-doors as well as indoors, is alert to potential physical hazards. She places herself strategically near climbing apparatus, assessing the skill and potential of each child. She warns about dangerous use of equipment, demonstrates safe ways of arranging boards for sliding, walking or bouncing.

She is aware that the out-of-door play time is a great releaser of energy, an active muscle builder as well as a developer of good coordination. She is also aware that the out-of-door play-time can offer opportunities for dramatic play, and for quiet sensory play with sand and water, dirt and mud. Creatures are part of outdoor discoveries: worms, insects, butterflies, cocoons. The magic of seeds and what happens when you plant them provides a kind of learning that books can't convey. It takes so long to grow!

Seasonal changes: the leather leaves of oak trees, the lacy leaves of maples, leaves to rake and toss and tumble in. Snow, feathery and soft and cold; spring rains and buds and soft greening—these are all part of the child's outdoors, and his teacher is the revealer of their magic.

Daily Routines
and Group Experiences

Although play is the core of the curriculum of good nursery schools, and teacher's energies and attention must be focussed on providing the best possible conditions for play, there are also routine facts of nursery school life that must be considered and planned for.

The way in which these routines are managed reflects the relative importance they hold in the total planning scheme. Cleaning up, putting away toys, toileting, washing, juice procedures are all part of everyday living in the nursery school. Obviously they offer little creative potential, but they deserve the kind of organization that will result in casual and effective functioning.

There have been varying degrees of emphasis on these routines over the years. There have been times when they, rather than play, seemed to be the core of curriculum planning. Most of the child's day was filled with energy-consuming attention to their correct fulfillment. I have observed nursery schools where children were greeted with cups of water (liquid intake), then steered to the toilet (liquid output), then put on cots for preplay rest. Play seemed grudgingly wedged into the more important activities of eating, washing, toileting and resting.

Today's emphasis on these routines is generally more casual. In relation to toileting, the teacher remains alert to signs and signals of individual children and reminds them to go to the toilet. She is fortunate if the bathroom is adjacent to the playroom, so that she can give help if it is needed. In less convenient situations, she may need to plan organized group toileting times for those who need it. It is usually a good idea to remind the children to go to the bathroom before getting into heavy outdoor clothing, when children are preparing to go outside. Some children may need frequent reminders, some children may be completely independent, some may not need to go to the bathroom during the morning, some may be actively resistant to using a toilet away from home.

It is usually helpful to the teacher to get information from the mother of each child about her child's characteristic toileting pattern, and to follow it as carefully as she can. Casualness is the key attitude to seek and foster. This is not always easy with children for whom toileting has been a battleground fraught with tension between mother and child.

"Accidents" also deserve to be treated with casual acceptance. As the teacher cleans up the child (standard equipment should include extra panties and socks for every child) she will remind him that he needs to tell her when he has to go to the toilet, and that she will always help him.

Washing hands is another routine that teachers need to provide for. The teacher with an exaggerated sense of cleanliness may insist on a formal ritual of soaping and rinsing after toileting and before juice as well as after using some of the messier materials such as paint, dough, paste, or clay.

In the not so olden days, half-day nursery school bathrooms were ringed with individual washcloths and towels hanging from hooks. In a university nursery school, in which I observed, the washing up period was conducted by the nurse (symbol of antisepsis) who stood in the doorway and chanted a washing-up ritual. The children responded in a seeming hypnotic daze. They undoubtedly emerged clean, but I question the value of spending twenty minutes to a half hour on something that might have been adequately accomplished in a few minutes.

The opposite extreme is the "dirt can't hurt" attitude of some teachers who don't even seem to see it, and except for major emersions in paint or mud or plastics, tolerate it.

There should be a middle ground characterized neither by toleration of grime, nor glorification of cleanliness. This middle-ground teacher will encourage casual wash-ups or "splash-ups" at low child-height sinks, under running water which rinses as it cleans. Liquid soap from a dispenser and paper towels constitute adequate equipment. A casual suggestion, "It might be a good idea to wash your hands now," is just as effective as the elaborate ritual which needs a conductor, and consumes most of the morning hours.

Putting away toys and play materials is another routine part of nursery school life which the teacher needs to consider.

Again, there are extremes of attitude and practice among nursery school teachers. There are those who insist that the termination of each activity be followed by immediate and proper putting away of materials before another activity is started. Each child is held accountable for his materials and their return to the proper place. This attitude results in a tidy classroom, but it has some limitations. I have seen children who have refused to build with blocks because they didn't want to pay the price of having to put them away. If this attitude of tit-for-tatness is carried to an extreme, as it tends to be, it puts a damper on creativity or even zestful exploration and discovery. "Neatness is all" as a classroom motto stultifies rather than releases.

The opposite attitude of "anything goes" or "leave it be" results in a hodgepodge of disorder that prevents creative use and enjoyment of materials. When blocks are scattered all over the floor, no one can build; when tables are cluttered with scattered puzzle pieces, mixed with pasting materials and dough or clay, no satisfying activity can take place there. Books should not be tossed carelessly around the room. Such treatment is not only damaging to books, but builds into children a kind of disrespect for books that should not be permitted to develop. Doll corners should be lived in with the kind of disorder that comes from active dramatic use, but should not be allowed to become a muddled mess of scattered toys and props.

Frequently teachers who promote this kind of chaotic scene do so with the best intentions. They feel that by insisting that children share in the cleaning up and putting away of materials, they are interfering with the child's constructive impulses.

Again I feel that there is a reasonable middle ground that permits and encourages creative use of materials and also teaches respect for them. Children can be helped by casual reminders to return one book or puzzle to the shelf before taking another. Or they can be reminded that they should use the blocks they have taken from the shelf before getting another pile.

In most nursery schools there is a general cleaning up or putting away time at the end of the work-play period. Children can be helped to participate in this. Sometimes it helps to assign specific areas to children, not necessarily because they have been engaged in that area. Picking up the block area is usually the most difficult, but this can be organized in a variety of ways. If the teacher piles the blocks of similar sizes, children can stack them on the shelves. Or children may be assigned a certain size or shape which will be their job. "Bob will be the cylinder loader." "Jill will be the animal and people loader." Sometimes singing the "piling song"—"Pile the blocks in even rows, Stephen knows where each one goes," inserting each child's name as it is repeated—is a pleasing accompaniment to clearing the block area.

When the job is completed, there should be a happy satisfied sense of accomplishment for everyone who has shared in it. "We really worked hard!"

To rest or not to rest in an official lying-on-mats-or-cots in the middle of the morning has been a somewhat controversial part of nursery school programs. The trend seems to be toward providing a quiet time of looking at books or listening to music rather than a formal lying on mats or rugs. Those of us who struggled with enforcement of the official lie-down rest period remember how unrestful it could be for those children who actively resisted it. Often it seemed to consume more energy than it restored. The mechanics of getting out individual mats (which usually occupied valuable storage space), putting them down, separating children of combustible potential, maintaining (policing) quiet atmosphere, and then after a suitable interval reversing the process often seemed to produce more tension than peace.

A more casual quiet time, a shift from active to passive activities, looking at books or pictures or a special exhibit of leaves or shells or something brought from home, a shift in pace seems more relaxing than an official lie-down period. We have found that the child who really needs to rest will quietly curl up or stretch out for a few minutes of relaxation without needing to have an official rest period in which to do it.

Following the busy work and play period and the clean-up time, it is a good idea to give a toileting and hand-washing reminder, before gathering for the snack and juice time that follows.

As in other routines, the juice time may have a wide range of "flavors." In some nursery schools it is a very formal affair. Juice is served by the teacher; crackers may be passed by her or a selected child, or placed on the napkin near the juice. In some schools a simple grace may be said. After finishing the snack, children are reminded to wipe their mouths, tuck the napkin in the cup, place the cup on the tray, and then go to the story group or whatever activity follows juice.

In one school that I observed, there seemed to be no structure to the juice time. A snack table apart from the work tables was set up with a pitcher of juice or milk and a basket of crackers. Children were informed of its presence. They came to it, received a cup of juice poured by the teacher, helped themselves to crackers, wandered off, eating and drinking wherever they happened to be. This method seemed too casual and shapeless. There was considerable spilling of juice en route, and crumbled crackers paved the floor.

Enthusiasm for children pouring their own juice seems to have subsided somewhat. However, if pitchers small enough to be successfully handled by three- and four-year-old hands are available, and children are helped to master the skill of pouring, it can be an enjoyable experience.

Since most eating situations involve sitting down, it seems reasonable to expect that juice time will be a sitting down rather than a wandering around occasion. It can also be a pleasant social occasion, a time for talking about things of interest to the group; something that happened on the way to school, something interesting that is going to happen, a trip, a current event of interest, plans for cooking. The teacher oftens needs to start the conversational ball, but she will be quick to take her cue from the children. Her goal is that the whole procedure will be a pleasant, enjoyable occasion. She will not fuss about manners, but she will demonstrate good manners herself. She will be gracious in thanking the child who passes the crackers, or she will politely ask for more if she wants more. She will comment favorably on children who do the same, not merely because it pleases her, but because it sounds pleasant and makes people feel good.

She will discourage disruptive behavior, deliberate juice spilling and cracker crumbling, as inappropriate and disturbing. She knows how contagious this can be, and how destructive to a happy snack time.

Some teachers are ingenious in varying the standard cracker and juice menu by introducing an assortment of raw fruits and vegetables, carrot and pepper sticks, apple quarters, tangerines and oranges, raisins, cereal. It is also fun for children to prepare special snack treats such as jello, cut-up fruit, cookies, salads, puddings, even soups. Many of these can be prepared without an elaborately equipped kitchen. They provide interesting experiences in learning about the nature and variety of food products, as well as good nutritional experiences.

To the uninitiated observer of a nursery school classroom, the lack of organized group times is often puzzling. It may be difficult for all observers to understand that important learning is going on in a room where each child is engaged in his own individual project. Their idea of a schoolroom is one where children are sitting down quietly and listening to the teacher, or following her directions.

Skilled nursery school teachers would be uneasy in such a classroom. They respect the needs of three- and four-year-olds to move about freely, and do not belittle the learning that takes place in a classroom of "movers." However, they also recognize that young children can be helped to enjoy brief "group times."

The juice or snack time is one of these. The story time and music time are other periods when the group assembles to share an experience.

In planning her day, the teacher will decide on the best time for these group experiences, usually a period immediately preceding or following the juice and snack time.

The mechanics of managing the group time are important. Shall the children sit in chairs or on the floor? Shall the children scramble for places, or be assigned special places? Where shall the teacher sit, on the children's level, or above them? What does the teacher do about potential disrupters of the peace? What about children who choose not to join the group? Should they be ignored or made to join? How does the teacher catch the attention of sixteen wiggling four-year-olds, and even more wiggling three-year-olds?

There is no standard set of rules that will guarantee success in managing a group story or music time. Each teacher has to discover her own characteristic way. Some teachers feel at home on the floor; others feel more comfortable sitting on a chair with children clustered at their feet. Some teachers like to have children seated in chairs; others feel that chairs complicate the situation or make it too formal.

The teacher with insight is not likely to insist that every child join the group the first time. She will respect the individual child who seems reluctant to join. However, she will not permit him to engage in activities that are disturbing and distracting to the group. She also has confidence that eventually he will be attracted to the group activity, and that his watching will not be wasted. She will quickly spot the combinations of children that stimulate disruption rather than participation, and she will separate them or arrange to have them near an adult who can help them.

She may begin (as Miss Bates did) by singing a simple song like, "Here we are together, together, together, Here we are together, all sitting on the floor. There's Billy and Buffy, and Timmy and Mary . . . (naming each child). Here we are together, all sitting on the floor." A song about shoes and sneakers, and who is wearing what color, is a sure way of catching the attention of shoe-conscious three-year-olds. Each child needs to hear his shoe or shirt described, and needs to hear his name. At first, this kind of singing tends to be a teacher solo, but as children catch on to it, they will join in and add to it.

Some teachers use finger plays as devices for capturing and holding group attention. Children seem to enjoy these action games as well as simple circle games like *Punchinello* and *Here*

We Go, Sandy Maloney. They enjoy initiating the action in answer to the question, "What can you do, Punchinello, little fellow, what can you do, Punchinello, little dear?" Imitating Punchinello's choice of "doing" is equally delightful.

Many nursery school teachers who lack musical skills are reluctant to include music in their programs. The teacher who can play the piano certainly has an advantage over those who cannot. But there are simple instruments such as the autoharp and the recorder which can be mastered without an extensive musical background. The autoharp in particular provides a pleasant chord accompaniment to singing. Drum beats can substitute for piano accompaniment to rhythms—fast beats, slow beats, running beats, skipping beats. Singing-action games like *The Little Gray Pony* need no accompaniment except the singing voice or a drum beat.

Sometimes parents with musical skills can be recruited to share them with the group. A guitar-playing mommy or daddy is a welcome addition to any group.

The group music time, like the story time, should be an optional affair. There are often some children who seem reluctant to join the group, but who may watch and listen from a distance. The teacher accepts this watching-listening as a preliminary to participation. She knows that a happy group experience is usually irresistible, and that eventually each child will join it when he is ready.

The preschool group or "together" time needs to be an experience which children can enjoy, and from which they can learn some of the simple rules of being members of a group: the responsibilities of not disturbing the group activity, of contributing to the group enjoyment, of listening and responding appropriately. Early group times should be brief, and timed to end before they disintegrate. The teacher is the stage manager, the mood setter, and the terminator. If she enjoys it, the children are likely to enjoy it, too.

Nursery schools and day care centers with all-day programs have the additional and essential routines of the noon meal and the afternoon nap to plan for. These are important routines which require special equipment as well as storage space. They also deserve the thoughtful planning of teachers, so that they will be enjoyable occasions rather than hectic and harried, or rigid lock-step routines.

The lunch period should be an occasion for the enjoyment of good food in a social situation. I can remember my first experience as an assistant teacher in an all-day program. Lunch was rolled into the classroom on a wagon. Children (already bibbed) were lying on cots for a pre-lunch rest. Teachers served the plates and summoned the children to the tables. *Everything* on the plate had to be eaten before melba toast chunks were distributed (these were great favorites!) and finally dessert and milk. There was one particularly dismal meal which appeared weekly: a barely poached egg (the white still transparent) sitting on top of some dreary spinach. No one liked it, and one little girl finally refused to eat it. She sat stolidly before the offensive plate, quietly but firmly asserting, "I won't eat it. I hate it. It's not even cooked." The teacher finally removed the plate to the kitchen with the comment that it would be waiting for her after her nap.

After nap, Jill was escorted to the kitchen to be confronted with the cool mess of uncooked egg and spinach. She was told that she could return to the playroom after she had eaten it.

When she returned to the playroom, the teacher asked her if she had eaten her lunch. Jill answered, "Yes, and then I throwed it up." And she had!

Shepherd's pie was a favorite dish to most of the children. It was a sort of meat and vegetable stew baked with a biscuit topping. Peter liked all of it except the peas which he carefully excavated, one by one. At first he disposed of them by surreptitiously dropping them on the floor or putting them under his plate or in his pocket. Then he discovered that Marcia was an avid pea eater, so he was able to dispose of his pea pile, win Marcia's favor, and manage to clean the plate in a single operation. The teacher somehow missed this little pea exchange, and I (who was a student teacher) must admit that I did not draw it to her attention.

I like to think that this rigid kind of food service is no longer in vogue or practice. The whole point of serving food to children is that they will be exposed to a variety of nutritious foods, and learn to eat and enjoy them.

Miriam Lowenberg, a well-known nutritionist, makes a strong plea that parents and teachers respect the fact that young children require very small servings. I remember a demonstration that she once gave of actual servings that were nutritionally adequate, which shocked the attending parents. One quarter of a potato rather than a whole potato was considered an adequate portion for three-year-olds. She also pled for more legitimate "finger foods": lettuce in small pieces, raw vegetables, bacon. She recommended that soup be served in cups rather than spooned from bowls; dessert as an integral part of the meal, not a reward for eating the meat and vegetables; bite size servings; "pushers" of toast or a specially constructed utensil for loading spoons or forks.

Children should be encouraged but not forced to try new foods. "Take a little tastè. At first you may not like it because it is a new taste, but after a while you may like it very much."

Dr. Clara Davis's experiments with infants and young children in selecting their own diets have demonstrated that if children are presented with a variety of nutritious foods and are permitted to make their own choices over a period of time, they will choose a well-balanced diet. She showed that children often go on food "jags," eating large quantities of a single food item. This is nothing to be alarmed about. It often represents an organic need to which the child is unconsciously responding.

In some of the early research centers, elaborate and detailed studies were made of children's eating habits. Every mouthful of food was recorded, as well as food which was rejected. I'm not sure what was learned. But the atmosphere around the luncheon tables was hushed and unnatural as teachers checked off intake and refusals.

Today the lunch period is a more relaxed and casual affair. Children are served small portions of the day's menu. They may return for "seconds" if they wish, or exchange their plates for dessert. There is a pleasant atmosphere of enjoying the food and the occasion. Table manners are not stressed, although unattractive behavior is discouraged. Food is to be tasted or eaten, not thrown on the floor. Spitting out food is not encouraged. Proper use of utensils is encouraged, but legitimate "finger-food" eating is also permitted. Teachers are not dismayed by refusals or accidental spills, nor do they expect children to eat at the same rate of speed. There will be speedy eaters and pokey eaters, just as there are among adults. Children who have finished eating are permitted to leave the table, wash off food remnants from hands and face, then go to their cots to look at books or start their rest.

Nursery schools which have space enough to have a separate sleep room are fortunate. Most schools have to convert the play space into sleeping space, by hauling in cots and screens, and fitting them into the space. This is harder to manage, but it can be done, and done well.

The teacher soon learns which children are ready to nap and need little or no help in relaxing and getting to sleep. She also learns the ones who resist nap, who are potential disturbers of the peace, and she tries to place these in strategically "safe" zones. Some teachers begin the nap period by playing some quiet music, or they may tell or read a story or sing some gentle tunes. Some teachers may have a "signal" that announces the official beginning of nap time, the flicking off of the light or drawing the shades. Some teachers tiptoe around the room, patting or tucking in each child. A particularly restless child may need a teacher to sit beside him. One teacher that I know took a nap herself, after the last child had been tucked in!

Getting up from nap is another routine that presents the teacher with a management problem. However, not all children will be ready to get up at the same moment. The short nappers can be helped first, shoes tied, blanket folded and stowed away, cot removed to storage. Gradually the room is restored to its play space appearance and usage, as sleepers awake and resume their afternoon activities.

The important thing about all routines of nursery school life is that they be conducted in a casual way. The teacher's attitude will determine their nature and quality. If she is tense and rigid about them, her attitude will be reflected by tension and resistance in the children. If her attitude is loose and shapeless, routines will be equally loose and shapeless, and so will the children's behavior. If she sustains a spirit of sprightly clarity, this too will be reflected in the children's acceptance of them as a part of their nursery school day. Routines can be genial learning situations, or hectic periods of resistance and confusion. The teacher sets the tone by her attitude toward them. She neither glorifies them nor denies their importance. By accepting them herself, she helps her children to accept them matter-of-factly.

Books and Stories

I used to think that any story to which children gave their spontaneous attention was suitable for them. I've changed my mind about this after having observed children giving their attention to stories that seemed in no way suitable for them. A friend of mine used to read from a highly scientific journal to his four-year-old son. Alex listened with seeming attentiveness. Amy used to listen with apparent raptness to her grandfather's reading of Latin poetry. And I have observed young children seemingly entranced with the dramatic reading of a horror tale by a well-intentioned baby sitter who was enjoying the story herself, and who was also pleased at the quality of attention it inspired in her listeners.

The fact that children listen is not sufficient evidence of the interest or suitability of the story material. The child who listened to his father's scientific journals was not necessarily a precocious scientist in the making. It is more likely that he enjoyed the company and attention of his father, the coziness of sitting in his lap and having him all to himself. This pleasure was worth the price of listening to unintelligible reading. And Amy, who listened to her grandfather reading Virgil, may have enjoyed the sonorous sounds, but it is more likely that she enjoyed the sole attention of grandfather.

We know that children may give their attention to stories

that may not necessarily be suitable or good for them, just as they may select food that is not good for them, or experiences that are dangerous but appealing, or toys that are flashy but fragile. The perceptive adult, the teacher or the parent, needs to select the books and stories that will be suitable and enjoyable. How do we decide what is suitable or unsuitable?

Let us look at the clues which children give us. What kinds of stories do young children give their *real* attention to? Which stories stimulate questions, comments, laughter? Which stories make eyes shine, and bring the response, "Read it again!" Which are the stories to which children give only partial attention? Which stories produce expressions of concern, confusion, or fear?

Let us see if we can define or describe unsuitable story material. First, we need to realize that unsuitable is not the same as bad. Stories that are unsuitable for three-year-olds may be highly suitable for five- or six-year-olds. Suitability of a story may be described with reference to the age and stage of development of the child to whom it is offered. Stories have a kind of intellectual and emotional digestibility that determines their suitability at any level. I remember my first reading of Lucy Sprague Mitchell's classic story *How Spot Found a Home*[34] to a group of young four-year-olds. This is a story of suspense and strong feelings. Poor little Spot has no home, and he is sharply rejected in his attempts to find a home. "Scat, scat, you old street cat, scat, scat, and never come back"! says the old woman as she brandishes her broom at him. It ends well with Spot finding a home with two children and lots of saucers of milk. The children were extremely attentive to the story. There were audible sighs of relief at the happy ending, except for Lilian who burst into tears and announced that she never wanted to hear that story again, and she wanted to go home.

Spot was a good story, but for some reason it was not "suitable" or good for Lilian at that moment. For weeks she shuddered when she saw the outside of the book in which Spot resided.

I think there has been a tendency in the past to force upon children and young people a literary fare beyond their power to comprehend or appreciate or "digest." This has resulted in being able to say that you have read the book or heard the

story, even though you know you have not savored it to its
fullest. I was always grateful that I did not meet Dickens until
I was in college. I couldn't possibly have enjoyed *David Copper-
field* as fully as I did then, had I been forced to read it earlier.

Stories of the unfamiliar or the technical are unsuitable for
young children. Stories about child life in Jakarta seem less
suitable for a three- or four-year-old than stories about child
life in his own home town. Stories about the techniques of
spacecraft flights seem less appropriate than a simple story
about a little boy whose daddy was an astronaut. Stories about
bizarre animals that never lived seem more confusing than il-
luminating. Frightening stories confuse rather than clarify.

Lucy Sprague Mitchell was a pioneer story writer of the "Here
and Now" school of writing. Her stories were based on real life
experiences rather than fantasy or faraway events and places.
She felt strongly that young children are still actively engaged
in sorting out what's real from what's unreal, and stories are
one of the ways in which they do this. She maintained that
the child must be sure of what's real before he can feel safe
with the unreal and fantastic. She wrote, "The attempt to amuse
children by presenting them with the strange, the bizarre, the
unreal is the unhappy result of adult blindness. Children do
not find the unusual piquant until they are firmly acquainted
with the usual; they do not find the preposterous humorous
until they have intimate knowledge of ordinary behavior; they
do not get the point of alien environments until they are securely oriented in their own."[34]

Mrs. Mitchell's firm stand on the importance of the "Here
and Now" as a basis for story materials for young children did
not imply condemnation of all fairy, folk, and fantasy story material. It merely emphasized postponement of the fantasy material until the child was sufficiently rooted in reality, so that he
could distinguish comfortably between fact and fantasy. The very
young child is busy building his world of reality. Until he is
certain about what is real, he may accept real and unreal without discrimination. It is hard for us to understand that very
young children cannot always distinguish between what is real
and what is pretend.

Parents and teachers sometimes ask, "But what's the matter

with 'Little Red Riding Hood' and 'Jack and the Bean Stalk' and 'Three Billy Goats Gruff'? I loved goblins and wolves and giants and witches when I was little. I want my children to enjoy them."

The fact which they may not recall is *when* they enjoyed these classic fairy and folk tales. Six-year-olds and some five-year-olds may enjoy these tales, because by then they can be sure of their pretend quality. They have lived long enough to be reasonably sure that wolves don't really behave like the one who ate grandmother. Furthermore, they may feel certain that wolves are not likely to be wandering around loose. They can feel free to enjoy the suspense of "Jack and the Beanstalk" because they know that beanstalks don't really grow to the sky, and that even if they did, no giant would climb down it, because giants are pretend, not real.

I recall a story told to me by the mother of a sensitive four-year-old child who reported a persistent terrifying dream after having listened to the reading of the "Three Bears." In Ellen's dream, when Goldilocks was found by the three bears in the baby bear's bed, she jumped out of bed, ran downstairs—but, unlike Goldilocks in the story, who ran out of the door into the woods until she reached her own home, in Ellen's dream, Goldilocks couldn't get out of the bear's house! The doors and windows were shut tight, and Goldilocks could not escape. She was trapped in the house with the angry bears! And Ellen awoke screaming.

It is quite possible that the story of the "Three Bears" was not the cause of Ellen's anxiety dream, but it surely triggered it, and seemed to increase rather than diminish her anxiety.

Bears are real, not like ghosts and witches and giants. And the situation in which Goldilocks found herself could be imagined as happening to *you*, if you are a sensitive, imaginative three- or four-year-old. If you are a sturdy five- or six-year-old when you first hear the story, you can shiver appreciatively at the danger of Goldilocks, but you know it will turn out all right, because it's only a pretend story, not a true one.

Katharine Read, the nursery educator, agrees with Mrs. Mitchell that the function of books and stories for the young child should be to recreate the world he knows, and thereby strengthen his understanding of it. She, too, feels that fanciful unreal stories are better left until the child has had time to form a sound concept of what the real world is like. The educators and parents who resist this point of view maintain that the factual "Here and Now" story is dull and unimaginative. They are bored by such stories, and assume that children are also bored.

But these stories are not always boring to children. Even strictly informational stories are appealing to children who are eager to learn the facts. I remember reading Lois Lenski's *Little Airplane* to a group of four-year-olds. As I encountered some rather technical descriptive terms of parts of the plane, I found myself omitting the terms and inserting simpler terms. At one point, one of the children confronted me somewhat sternly, "What's the matter? Can't you read? It says that's the aileron!" I realized that the terminology was important to this four-year-old who had a strong interest in airplanes. What seemed over-technical to me was of genuine interest to him. He wanted to hear the correct terms.

I must admit that after thirty years of reading Lois Lenski's stories about the Little Family, the Little Auto, the Little Fireman, and all the rest of her little characters and events, I find them somewhat lacking in sprightliness and adventure. But that doesn't mean that three- and four-year-olds do not still find them satisfying. I have never failed to elicit a warm response from three-year-olds listening to a reading of *The Little Family*. Head noddings of approval and understanding accompany each page. "*My* daddy goes to work, too!" "I had toast for breakfast, too!" It is more than just a me-too-ness response. It is a comfortable corroboration of "that's the way my world is, and it's good to hear about it."

Not all "Here and Now" stories need to be strictly factual descriptions of events or processes familiar to young children. They can be flavored with humor and suspense. There can even be stories with distortions of the known and familiar. These provide enjoyment as well as practice in distinguishing real from pretend.

I remember the story that Jessie Stanton once told a group of five-year-olds at the Vassar Summer Institute about the cow who didn't want to go to school. She described the cow getting out of bed in the morning, going to the bathroom to brush her teeth and wash her face, taking off her nightgown and putting on her panties and her dress and socks and shoes. "She had a hard time tying her hair ribbons on her horns. Then she went downstairs to breakfast. She had orange juice and cereal and toast and milk, but no marmalade."

The children, who had just returned from a trip to the farm where they had learned a great deal about cows and their way of life, looked somewhat puzzled as the story began. They knew that cows lived in barns, not houses; that they slept in stanchions, not beds; that they ate hay, not toast and cereal. And because they knew these cow facts of life, they could enjoy the genial distortion of these facts. They began to add to the story, and it ended hilariously. It was a silly story, a funny pretend story with no danger of confusion, since the children were sure of their cow facts.

There seem to be certain story themes that are perennially appealing to young children. These are stories about the known and familiar which corroborate their own experiences, stories which inform and clarify, stories with a hint of mystery which is always resolved, stories which echo their own feelings, stories which convey a mood. The following titles are examples of some of these major literary themes.

Caps for Sale, by Esphyr Slobodkina, is a classic humor story. And even our modern urban and suburban children, who are not familiar with traveling pedlars, who buy their caps in a department store, and who are not accustomed to seeing a treeful of monkeys, can still get the humor of the monkeys imitating the pedlar and the final trick by which he retrieves his caps.

The Runaway Bunny, by Margaret Wise Brown, is a story with a gentle magic quality. Finding the runaway bunny as he assumes his disguises as a flower in the garden, a fish in a stream, a cloud in the sky, a rock on the mountain is part of the fun. Knowing that the mother bunny will always find him is wonderfully comforting and reassuring. Children know that the bunny couldn't really become all the things he threatens to become. They know it is all beautiful make-believe, and they love it.

Stories with an element of suspense or mystery are hard to find on this early childhood level. *Hurry, Hurry,* by Edith Thatcher Hurd, is a good one in this category. Mrs. Smith's succession of disasters, which she brings upon herself by her terrible need to hurry, are delightfully anticipated by repeated warnings that something worse might happen if she didn't stop hurrying—"and something worse *did* happen!"

Stories of hiding, like *Where Is Andy?* by Jane Thayer, provide a delicious bit of suspense, as do stories of lost objects or animals or people who always are found in the end. The "Noisy" books, by Margaret Wise Brown, have a tantalizing note of mystery, of guessing what it was that Muffin heard or saw or felt, as well as a rich assortment of sensory impressions that stimulate thinking.

Leopard on a String, by Ann Kirn, is an amusing switch on the lost animal theme. This lost leopard, who has terrified the sheriff and all the townspeople, is found in the woods by a little boy who leads him back to his cage which is where he had wanted to be all the time!

The story of *Mike Mulligan, the Steam Shovel,* by Virginia Lee Burton, is another classic mix-up about the steam shovel who digs himself into a hole and then can't get out.

Lately there have been stories for young children involving situations and people with which children could identify emotionally. These are not moralistic tales of what happens when children will not brush their teeth, or go to bed, or eat their dinners properly. These are stories about little boys who get angry at their sisters, like *Willy Is my Brother* by Peggy Parish and Shirley Hughes; or children who get mad at each other, in *Let's Be Enemies* by Janice May Udry; *Go Away Dog* by Joan S. Nudset is another example of this type of story. These stories invite discussion and identification with the feelings they describe. Children who get into mischief, who get angry, who are afraid are beginning to find their way into stories; not just kittens who are timid, or cocker spaniels who are frisky and get into trouble.

"Mood" books are still another category of stories which are appealing to young children. Margaret Wise Brown's *Goodnight, Moon* sets a soothing sleepy tone which children enjoy. *The*

Night Mother Went Away, by Charlotte Zolotow, is a gentle story about a little girl whose daddy took her out of bed and into the night world of stars and moonlight. There is a quiet kind of magic in this kind of story which many children find very appealing. The plot is minimal. There is no climax, no suspense, but there is a feeling of tenderness and the magic of nighttime.

The form of a story for young children is also important. It need not be elaborate or complex. In fact, it needs to be simple, brief, without sub-plots. Mrs. Mitchell states that repetition is the simplest and one of the most pleasing patterns. Repetition of a phrase or rhythmic sounds capture and hold the interest of young children, like the refrain of the *Little Engine That Could:* "I think I can, I think I can, I think I can," as she laboriously climbs the mountain, and her joyous "I thought I could, I thought I could, I thought I could," as she rolls the trainload of toys cheerily down the mountainside.

Mrs. Mitchell also states that even the simplest relation of meaningful events in chronological sequence makes a satisfactory story for the very young. *Baby Ann,* by Lois Lenski, is nothing more than the relating of the events in Baby Ann's day, from her waking up in the morning until she goes to sleep at night. This may not seem exactly exciting in plot to the more sophisticated literary tastes of five- and six-year-olds. But to three-year-olds it makes a very satisfactory story.

Some teachers of young children seem reluctant or uneasy about reading poetry to young children. They may be willing to read or recite Mother Goose rhymes with which children are often familiar before they come to school. Even those with content having little relevance to the lives of today's children have a bouncy appeal because of their jingly rhythm and rhyme.

There are many good anthologies of poetry suitable for young children that are available today. *Poems to Read to the Very Young,* edited by Josette Frank, is one of them. Simple themes about baths and birthdays and going to bed, about animals and nature have a genuine appeal when put into simple rhyming. Reading poetry to young children can be an introduction to the world of poetry which is so often neglected in adult living. Children enjoy hearing the same poems read over and over again. Frequently children will memorize poems with which they have become familiar, not because the teacher set out to teach them, but because they enjoy the lilt and rhythm and sound.

The teacher has an important role not only in selecting stories and poems which are appropriate and enjoyable for her children, she also has a responsibility in fostering proper care and use of books. Books should be kept on a rack or shelf available to children. They should be kept in good repair. Torn pages or bindings should be mended promptly. Children should be encouraged to look at one book at a time, rather than gathering a pile which gets strewn about. If a library table is available it is wise to encourage its use. However, a cozy cushioned corner of the floor can be a pleasant retreat for looking at books. The teacher teaches respect for books by the way in which she handles them, and the respect she accords them.

Most teachers of young children today seem more comfortable in reading stories than in telling stories. The art of story-telling seems to be a lost one. It is the rare teacher who has confidence in her ability to capture and hold the attention of her children without the visible support of a book. Yet those who dare to tell rather than read report great satisfaction in seeing the response in each child's face, with no book between the teller and the listener.

It is important that teachers be familiar with the book or story they plan to read. It is essential that they enjoy it, if they wish the children to enjoy it. It is almost impossible for a teacher to disguise her feelings about a story. If she enjoys it, she will convey her enthusiasm to the children. If she finds it dull or pointless, the children will sense her lack of enthusiasm, and reflect it.

A good story, well told or well read, will stimulate comments or questions among its listeners. These are indicators of interest and should not be considered interruptions. I once observed a teacher reading a story about boats to a group of four-year-olds. At one point there was a description of a ferry boat. One little boy (who I later learned had recently been on a ferry boat) tried to tell the teacher and the group something important that he knew about ferry boats. The teacher coolly reminded him that he must not interrupt the story and continued to read. Later, she

seemed surprised when I commented that I hadn't considered it
an interruption, but rather evidence of interest which should be
encouraged, not discouraged. It is almost impossible for children
to sit silently listening to *Caps for Sale*. They need to imitate the
"SSSt SSSt, you monkeys you!" They need to put pretend caps
on top of their own heads, and to imitate the pedlar's motions.

The listening patterns of three- and four-year-olds are not
passive. A successful story time may be filled with verbal and
action responses to the story. These should be permitted and
welcomed so long as they do not disrupt the story.

Stopping the reading of the story to look at the illustrations
and to talk about them is also a way of strengthening and sustaining interest in the story itself. Occasionally discussion may
wander away from the story, but the teacher can always bring
it back by terminating the discussion and continuing the reading. "I'd like to hear more about your puppy some other time,
John. But now we need to find out what happens to Mr. Turtle."

A group story reading time needs to be a comfortable time,
with children seated either on the floor or in chairs so that they
can see the teacher and the book. Teachers need to be adept
at holding the book so that all children can see the illustrations.
Children who are reluctant to join the group should be helped
to be occupied in a quiet activity which will not disturb the
story listeners. If the activity is within listening range of the
story, frequently the nonlistener becomes a listener, because
he cannot resist the lure of the story.

The teacher may introduce the story by holding up the book
and asking if anyone knows what the story is about. She may
announce the title of the story. She reads with clear carrying
tones, and with moderate dramatic effects when it is appropriate. She invites participation. When children are not in a
listening mood, or the story is not "getting across," she terminates
the story time matter-of-factly, not punitively. "I think I'll not
read any more of this story. It doesn't seem to be very interesting to you. Maybe we can try it again some other day."

The teacher usually chooses the story to be read. Her choice
is often influenced by something that is of current classroom
interest. A story about cats may follow the visit of a home cat;
a turtle story may appropriately highlight the acquisition of a

class turtle; a steam shovel story may follow a trip to observe
a neighboring excavation; a birthday story may add to the cele-
bration of the birthday child of the day.

Sometimes children will choose favorite stories to be reread.
And often stories are read just for fun and enjoyment, not in
relation to any particular event, or to teach any particular lesson.

The teacher is often confronted with books brought from
home which are unsuitable or inappropriate for group use. She
has the choice of presenting a modified version of the story
(which may not be acceptable to the owner) or of merely showing the pictures and talking about them, but not reading it. She
may manage to suggest that it is a better "home book" than
school book, without condemning it. She may be able to read it
to the child who brought it, and explain that it isn't so good for
the group, because they might not understand it too well. She
will discourage the bringing of such books from home.

Good stories, well read or told, can stimulate a love of literature in young children that will continue into their school years.
A four-year-old story-lover announced, "When I get old, I'm
going to have a library full of books, all kinds! Books about
machines and doctors and chipmunks and nature and fishes.
I'm even going to write some books myself. That's because I'll
be an author. I think I'll write one now! It's going to be a book
about the Frost Family. 'Once there was a very chilly family,'
that's the beginning. There was Mr. Frost and Mrs. Frost, and
of course, Jack Frost!"

It *was* a shivery story full of frosty feelings. Anthony is "old"
now (he is thirty-five). He *has* a library full of all kinds of books,
and he himself has begun to write. I like to feel that some of
this is related to the intense interest he developed in books and
stories as a preschooler, and the extent to which these interests
were stimulated by his teacher.

Classroom Atmosphere

The teacher sets the "stage" of her classroom through her selection of materials, her arrangement of them, and the invitations for work and discovery which they issue. The teacher not only sets the stage, she sets the tone, the flavor and quality of living and learning which goes on in her classroom. I shall try to describe three of these "tones," which have been variously labeled by observers and educators. The labels themselves are less important than the feelings and actions they engender.

The first one I shall describe is the one that has sometimes been called "authoritarian." In this kind of classroom the teacher is the boss, and there is no doubt about it. It is her voice that is heard when one enters the classroom, not the children's voices. Children are likely to be sitting quietly, following the teacher's directions in making identical constructions or pictures. Or they may be playing circle games, again under the careful instruction of the teacher. There is usually a strong emphasis on a correct procedure in routines, lining up for the bathroom, handwashing, etc. The time and opportunity for "free play" is limited and hemmed in with restrictions.

To the casual viewer or the inexperienced observer this kind of classroom may seem very appealing. It is quiet; children seem busy; the teacher is clearly in charge. It even looks like good teaching. It is not ugly or unpleasant, but it is flat, dull, and empty.

This kind of teaching requires little imagination, or sensitivity to individual differences or needs. A loud voice, a firm hand, and the imposition of her ideas on the children are the tools of the teacher. She has learned to trick or trap the children into compliance, often through threats and fear. With the tough ones, she gets tougher, bears down enough to corral and subdue them. This kind of education starts with the teacher, and it usually ends with the teacher. The children are incidental instruments through which she achieves her goal: fifteen more or less identical pumpkin pictures to take home at Hallowe'en.

This too-rigid tone of a teacher-dominated and directed classroom is a stultifying atmosphere for learning. It is a "skinny" kind of education. It deprives children of the opportunity to discover the delights of pumpkin-making on their own four-year-old terms (see Chapter 7). It is building toward nothing except continued reliance on adult telling and showing, and adult models to be copied. It is an effective deterrent to the discovery of one's own abilities and interests and delights, as well as one's particular creative talents and skills. It builds conformity; it discourages creativity. It stifles questions and curiosity.

The opposite of the authoritarian or teacher-imposed tone of classroom atmosphere is the "laissez-faire," or "anything goes" tone. The atmosphere of a classroom dominated by this tone is loose, shapeless and often child-dominated. The teacher permits, endures, and the result is chaos.

This exaggeratedly child-centered atmosphere is often the result of well-intentioned efforts of educators to avoid the too rigid patterns of authoritarian teaching. In their eagerness to avoid *repression,* these teachers have exalted *expression* out of all proportion to reality or the needs of children. They have swung from excessively rigid to excessively permissive atmospheres, and the result is chaos and bedlam.

Let us take a look at this permissive nursery classroom. What does it look like, how does it sound, what is happening?

First, it is usually deafeningly noisy; not just the busy hum of active children, but jumbled shrieks and roars. Often the victrola is blaring while one child attempts to listen, or no one listens. There is no evidence of a plan or design of the space or the objects or activities within it. There seem to be no limits, except prevention of serious injury to others. Materials are used chaotically. Clay or dough is tossed around, walked into, smeared. Paint covers shoes, clothing and walls, as well as people. Blocks are scattered throughout the room. Water is everywhere. Juice time is a shambles of crumbled crackers and spilled juice. Story-time is a trial of endurance against the multiple noisy activities of children who wander about disrupting the listeners. At least two children are usually engaged in a jolly but totally incon-siderate free-for-all interference program, mischievously knocking down buildings and disturbing other children's activities, or just running, hooting, and threatening. There are also usually some children wandering about in a kind of aimless, bewildered state. There are some children who seem able to shut out the chaos, to become absorbed in some activity, but most are unable to concentrate. It's not easy to sustain interest in the midst of such wildness.

Where is the teacher in this picture? She isn't often heard; she can usually be found attending one child. It is as if she set the stage for chaos and then withdrew. It isn't that she doesn't care what happens. She is actively engaged in sponsor-ing the kind of program which she believes is beneficial to the children. When things get too tangled, she may step in with a mild diversionary tactic. She is usually more comfortable out of doors than indoors. More space seems to absorb both the aimless activity and the thundering noise. In contrast to the too-rigid teacher who dominates her group, the permissive teacher is at the mercy of her group.

I cannot condone this kind of experience in the name of edu-cation. To me this is the poorest possible kind of preparation for what comes next in education or in life. This kind of atmo-sphere can only promote confusion, never clarity toward learning.

The third "tone" which I would like to describe is one which creates an atmosphere of order without regimentation. It is a classroom in which clarity and warmth prevail. There is an at-titude of mutual respect between children and teachers. Teachers listen to children; children listen to teachers. The teacher enjoys the children. She lets them know that she does, by her tone of voice, her facial expression, and her sharing of their delights. She accepts each child for himself. She does not expect uniformity of response or interest. She is alert to "readiness signals," and is responsive to them. She knows that a child who may be resistant to joining the "juice group" will probably one day show signs of wanting to be part of it. When she senses this, she may invite him to pass the crackers, or designate a special place for him at a nearby table. She won't overdo it, but she will rejoice quietly with him, with a smiling glance of recognition of his progress.

The teacher in this setting of democratic respect will not begrudge or belittle watching as an effective preliminary to action and participation. She never feels "He's *just* watching," nor will she feel the need to tease or force the child into action. She knows that watching is often an essential and effortful first step toward daring to do or be. She steers away from enticing him by asking questions like "Would you like to try it?" unless she is willing to accept a "No." But as she accepts his need to watch, she may issue the assurance that "Someday you might feel like doing it."

Our ideal nursery school is constantly issuing invitations that encourage the child's discovery of himself, and providing answers to "What's fun?," "What's hard?," "What's easy?," "What's scary?" After a year or two of exposure to this kind of teaching atmosphere, the child gains clarity about the ingredients of his own personality. A design begins to take shape. "I'm the kind of person who likes people (or who doesn't like people), whom people like (or don't like), who can do hard things (or can't do anything well), who gets mixed up, who is sometimes afraid." These feelings may be good or bad to live with.

The healthy, hearty, respectful nursery school is concerned with providing the kind of atmosphere which contributes toward the acquisition of positive feelings. It does this by encouraging the kind of behavior that makes for good feelings, and by limiting and disapproving of the kind of behavior that results in "bad" feelings.

The child who is permitted and thereby encouraged to build a picture of himself as the kind of guy who can beat up everybody in the school is encountering a real obstacle to his current and future healthy development.

This "tone" is a positive builder of attitudes toward work

and learning. It is one which issues multiple invitations for discovery of relationships and development of skills, through the equipment and materials it provides, and the way in which they are presented. Again, the teacher determines the nature of this presentation, and thereby the quality of learning and discovery that goes on in her classroom. She is the "stage-setter," and she is the tone-setter. She not only arranges her classroom with challenging materials, and keeps them in good working order, she encourages children to be resourceful in using the materials. This does not mean permitting misuse of materials, or presenting so many in a kind of indiscriminate clutter that children confront confusion rather than clarity. It means selecting and offering suitable materials, setting necessary and reasonable limits, offering help as requested, sharing each child's delight in achievement or discovery, giving no models to copy, and making no comparisons.

A nursery school with our "democratic" atmosphere offers the kinds of experiences which it considers to be educational and not just casually pleasant pastimes. It believes that it is actively teaching children, and that children are actively learning some very basic things, even though these learnings may seem somewhat remote from measurable academic skills.

It is engaged in teaching skills and concepts, not by requiring all children to produce the same product simultaneously, or by instructing in specific techniques, but by the richness and variety of raw materials which it offers children, and the opportunities for discovery which it provides.

It teaches attitudes, not by preaching or nagging or moralizing, but by demonstrating and encouraging the kinds of attitudes that make for harmony and understanding and tolerance. It teaches control of primitive impulses by clearly limiting and discouraging destructive behavior, and by offering acceptable substitutes as well as opportunities for discussion. It opens the doors of discovery of things and self by alerting children to the wonders of the everyday world, the joys and delights as well as the mysteries of the world around us. It is neither too rigid nor too permissive. It is human and caring.

Building Attitudes Toward Learning

Many years ago I observed an art lesson being taught to a kindergarten group. The lesson for the day was to draw a carrot. An 8 x 12 piece of manila drawing paper, and an orange and green crayon were placed before each child.

The teacher announced that today they would learn to draw the carrot. She asked the children to fold their hands in their laps, listen to her and follow her directions. She stood at the blackboard in front of the children, and with a piece of chalk drew a tapering mass of horizontal lines roughly indicating the shape of the carrot. She followed this with a flick of chalk at the upper end of the skinny inverted pyramid, apparently to represent the stem or leaf stalk. She then requested that the children imitate her drawing with their fingers in pantomime. Some children were able to follow this direction; others seemed bewildered. This airy wiggling of fingers was repeated until everyone participated. The next direction was to repeat the action on the paper, still with fingers, not crayons. After this had been practiced sufficiently, the children were told to pick up the orange crayon and draw the carrot in the manner of the airborne strokes. By this time at least one child had grabbed both crayons in his fist and assaulted the paper with vigorous scribbles. Most of the children tried to follow her directions, including the final fillip of green denoting the stem at the top.

145

The results were a collection of wavering elongations of orange, vaguely approximating the carrot they were aiming to resemble. There was no evidence of discovery or delight in their production. And I cannot feel that much had been learned about drawing the carrot. I suspect that this teacher felt that this had been a highly creative performance since she hadn't even given them identically outlined carrots to be filled in with color! She may even have thought that she was teaching something about the carrot itself.

How should the teacher have taught the carrot lesson to her group of four- or five-year-olds? First, I'm not at all sure she should have selected the carrot as an appropriate model for an art experience! If a single child had shown interest in representing carrots, she might have helped him to visualize them by talking about their shape, color, etc. She should certainly have tried to find a real carrot to look at, feel, and even nibble! But it seems unlikely that children this age would ever spontaneously select the carrot as a subject for art.

This does not mean that the carrot is not worthy of observation and study. In contrast to the foregoing description of carrots in art, I should like to describe a scene I observed in another four-year-old classroom where a group of children were about to embark on the project of preparing carrots for a snack.

Five or six children had gathered around the table. The teacher held up a bunch of carrots. "Do you know what these things are?" she asked. "Carrots," called out several of the children.

"That's right," said the teacher. "They are carrots." She handed one to each child. "What do they look like?"

"They look like carrots," said Andy.

Miss D. smiled and answered, "They really do, because they *are* carrots. What is the shape of them? Feel of them?"

"Mine is long and skinny," said Joe.

"Mine has a pointy end."

"Mine has hairs and circly rings."

"Do you know what color it is?" asked Miss D.

"Orange, like a carrot."

"What's on top of it?"

"Green stuff, like feathers and ferns," said Liz.

At this point Miss D. considered the possibility of continuing the discussion in the direction of the source of carrots, the nature of their growth, but decided to postpone this part of the learning for another day. She sensed there had been enough talk, and that action was needed.

She asked one more question—"What are carrots for, anyway?" And she received a loud group answer,

"For eating."

"That's right!" she replied.

"And sometimes cooking, too," added Betsy. "My mother cooks them."

"That's right, too. But before we eat them, we have to do something. Do you know what that is?"

This was a hard one, so Miss D. provided the answer, "We have to wash them, and we have to scrape the outside skin off."

Carrots were dumped in the basin of water she had provided, scrubbed with stiff brushes, dried on paper towels and then the process of scraping was begun. The teacher had brought some vegetable scrapers which were safe to use. This was tricky but challenging. Each child managed to acquire a little pile of carrot shavings which were given to the guinea pigs for their lunch. The scraped carrots were placed on a tray for snack time with a sense of satisfaction in accomplishment.

The teacher felt good about this introductory exposure to carrots, their nature and values. She planned, as a follow-up, a cooking experience with carrots to compare texture and taste with the raw vegetable. She also planned a series of investigations of other vegetables; peas, beans, onions, cauliflower, potatoes, possibly culminating in cooking a vegetable soup.

Her goal in presenting the vegetable series was not merely one of identification and proper nomenclature but of alerting her children to recognizing and describing essential qualities of things (vegetables). These were lessons in observation and description rather than mere identification. Through the subtle but perceptive guidance of the teacher, the children learned *about* carrots from carrots. The experience had been an enjoyable one, and a meaningful one. It had stimulated their powers of observation and challenged their ability to describe what they saw and felt. The experience had also served to sharpen their interest in the appearance and function of everyday objects. They had learned something about carrots from having a first-hand encounter with carrots under the lively direction of a teacher who saw the teaching as an experience rather than a lesson. She was able to convey more than carrot facts; she conveyed to the children something of her own enthusiasm and interest in the learning situation, even though the focus was only the humble carrot. Her hope was that they would carry this enthusiasm and interest to other learning situations whether they were vegetable, mineral, or human!

The role of the teacher in building positive attitudes toward learning and discovery is more easily observed and described when she is engaged in encouraging children to use materials creatively than when she is trying to teach social values. And yet the method is not so different. She teaches respect for materials by her arrangement of them, and by setting the stage for their best use. She accepts each child's individual approach. She discourages misuse of materials. She emphasizes the good feelings and the effort that accompany the activity, whether it is painting, block-building, clay, woodworking, or preparation of carrots for lunch.

Something of the same quality of concern and caring accompanies the teaching involved in helping children to acquire some of the social graces that will not only please their grandparents, but will make them agreeable, cooperative members of society. This is a more subtle kind of teaching. There are times when it seems more easily caught than taught. It is certainly not effectively taught by the lecture method, nor by trickery, bribery, ridicule, or threats.

Teachers of young children want to help them to learn about cooperating with others, about respecting the rights of others, and even about responding with appropriately gracious replies or actions to the friendly overtures or assistance of others. They know that these are hard lessons to learn, and that preschool children can only begin to learn them. They also know that they cannot be taught by drill or nagging. They are aware of the ineffectiveness of ridicule as a teaching method, as well as the corrosive effect of sarcasm. They are equally sure that words and gestures, however correct, are empty and meaningless if they are not accompanied by genuine feelings of concern and caring.

Most parents yearn to have their children acquire good manners, and many well-intentioned parents begin trying to bulldoze them into their children long before the children are able to understand their need or meaning. Some of these children manage to acquire a surface veneer of seeming courtesy. They learn the proper words and phrases, but without the feelings which should accompany them if they are to be genuine lubricators of social intercourse. The teaching of labels is insufficient. The child who mechanically mutters, "I'm sorry," after deliberately hurting another child needs help in knowing the true meaning of "I'm sorry." "But I said I'm sorry" is not enough.

Someone once remarked that true manners probably do not begin to be absorbed and practiced until about the time that permanent dentition takes place—at about age six or seven. This is a good thing to remember when trying to teach three- and four-year-olds.

In addition to the premature pressure that adults put upon young children to be polite and courteous, it has been my observation that many of these same adults are woefully lacking in courtesy toward the children they are trying to teach. "Shut the door!," "Give me the spoon," "Pick up the book!" are often delivered without benefit of the magic "Please" which is demanded of children's requests. The same adults neglect to say "thank you" or its equivalent when they have received a service from a child, and yet they demand the "thank you" from the child.

The early emphasis on labels rather than feelings sometimes "catches," but it does not necessarily result in courteous children. A three-and-a-half-year-old rushing out of a door into the hall bumped into another child. "I'm sorry," he muttered. "You're welcome," responded the victim.

A teacher once asked to borrow some scissors being shared by some four-year-olds engaged in a cutting and pasting project. "Callie, would you be kind enough to let me use your scissors?" she asked. Callie coldly replied, "You didn't say 'please.'"

At dressing-to-go-outside time, Debby, who had successfully gotten into and fastened her snowsuit and had put on her galoshes, was unable to manage the fasteners. She stuck her foot in the direction of the teacher and said with a kind of quiet desperation, "Miss B., will you please fasten these pesky things?" Miss B. responded with, "I'll be glad to help you, Debby. I'm always glad to help when people ask me in such a cheery way." Debby answered, "Well, that's because I've got those manners, *finally!* Thanks!"

"You're welcome," replied Miss B.

This little incident, more than an exchange of properly labeled pleasantries, was an exchange of genuine feelings of need, of recognition of the need, gratitude for meeting it, and mutual appreciation and caring. The intensity of Debby's "finally" also revealed that these graces are not easily learned.

Even learning to share is hard. It seems like such a simple concept to adults. We begin proclaiming the virtues of sharing long before children have any understanding of its meaning or merit. To young children it is more likely to mean giving up or losing a toy or a turn, rather than gaining one. One young four-year-old had his own interpretation of sharing. He approached the child in possession of the new dump truck which he wanted, and said, "In this school you're supposed to share, so you give me the dump truck, OK?"

Usually when the teacher confronts a child with the need to share, it is in terms of giving up. "Teddy, you've had a long enough turn on the swing. Now it's Sally's turn." From Teddy's point of view, he hasn't had a long enough turn. Some children may challenge the teacher's decision and refuse to release the swing. Others may attack the child selected to replace them.

There are devices that may help children to accept the pain of sharing. Setting a time limit on the use of a popular toy or activity sometimes helps. "Betsy, you may use the new tricycle for five minutes; then it will be Billy's turn. I'll tell you when it's time." These aids need to be carefully followed through, so that both the sharer and the "sharee" will learn that they can count on the fairness of the teacher.

The ultimate goal of helping children to manage sharing by themselves, without teacher intervention, maneuvering, or ref-ereeing, is harder to achieve. The good feelings that should be part of a shared experience need to be conveyed to children. The loser of the turn or the toy needs help in realizing that he is not just the loser, he is the *giver,* and that there is some pleasure in giving. This is a concept that is not entirely compatible with three-year-old needs and understanding; but persistent, patient demonstration can sometimes succeed in teaching it to four-year-olds. Most three-year-olds need to be convinced that release of a toy does not mean permanent loss. They also need many demonstrations of the return of the surrendered treasure before they are willing to "buy" this sharing business.

The teacher who is trying to teach that sharing is not just something that children are trapped and policed into accepting, but rather an action that has mutual satisfactions to those engaged in the encounter, is constantly alerted to spontaneous sharing situations uninitiated by the adults. When these occur, she is quick to point out their positive aspects. When Ellen voluntarily slipped out of the swing to give the waiting Trudy a turn, the teacher commented, "Ellen, that was so kind of you to give Trudy a turn on the swing." Ellen smiled, and it was clear to everyone that Trudy was pleased to be chosen by Ellen.

Capitalizing on such episodes, by pointing out the agreeable feelings engendered by such spontaneously gracious acts, is more effective teaching than the more negative pointing out of failures or omissions of grace.

Teachers teach attitudes toward others by their own attitudes of caring, of understanding, of sympathy, of enjoyment, and approval. They teach by casual demonstration. In their spontaneous responses to children, they are teaching the attitudes they hope their children will acquire. The teacher not only says, "Thank you" when a child hands her a cracker, she will add a smile to the words. When a child thanks her for help, she will respond with, "You are welcome. I'm glad I could help you."

It sometimes helps young children to have the adult say the gracious words aloud for them, rather than to demand that the children say the words. Then when the great day arrives when they say the "Thank yous" and "I'm sorrys," you can rejoice with them that they have learned to say the words that go with the feelings. If the feelings aren't there, the words are empty. Let's not teach our children emptiness in the name of graciousness and good manners.

Teacher-Child Relations

As one looks back on one's own school days, certain teachers remain vivid and sharp in one's memory. These are likely to be the "good" ones, those who shine out because they made learning exciting, or because they made themselves felt as real people, not just purveyors of subject matter. Or they will be the "bad" ones, those who tyrannically ruled the classroom with little regard for individual needs or differences, those who instilled fear of reprisal or ridicule for not producing the correct answer.

Any relationship may be defined as "an emotional connection between people." The nature of the emotional connection between teacher and child may be a positive one which promotes growth and learning, or it may be a negative one charged with suspicion and distrust, and accordingly one which obstructs growth and learning.

Since nursery school teachers are not limited by the need to teach academic subject matter, they are freer to develop a relationship with their children which is based on mutual respect and trust. This is something not readily learned or taught in the academic sense. It is something sensed or felt, and is not even too easy to describe when observed. It permeates the atmosphere of a classroom. It is the tone with which the teacher addresses the child, rather than the words she uses. It is subtle,

153

difficult to describe, more difficult to teach; yet it is the essential determinant of successful communication at any age level.

Children bring to their first school experience something of the feelings toward adults which they have acquired in their home-lives. If these experiences have been good ones, they will bring the same positive expectancies toward teachers which they have learned from adults at home. If these have been poor experiences, they will bring feelings of distrust and suspicion toward the new adult, the teacher.

But teachers bring a whole life-time of experience to their relationships with children. And their relationships with children will be a reflection of their own past relationships with crucial people in their own lives—their parents and family, and their teachers. The dominating, tyrant type of teacher relationship is likely to be the result of having experienced and resented the same kind of relationship as a child. It's as if teacher finally has a chance to assume the role to which she had to submit as a child.

I should like to try to describe some of the kinds of teacher-child relationships which I have observed. It is easy to describe the extremes. The one most obviously discernible is the teacher who rules her group with a strong hand and a loud voice. The children are her subjects. She is the "boss." The teacher dominates the classroom, controls by fear and sharpness. Children of such a tyrant-teacher are usually submissive (they had better be!), passive, seemingly accepting the harsh regime. They quickly learn not to challenge the teacher. They respect her power, but there is no feeling of respect for her or trust in her as a helping, caring person.

This tyrant quality of relationship is not only unpleasant, it is not a very healthy one for either the teacher or the child. It is likely to build strong feelings of fear and resentment in the child that will carry over into future classroom situations. It may also stimulate the development of feelings of his own unworthiness, since he receives no evidence from the teacher that he is valued.

The teacher who establishes this kind of relationship probably should not be working with young children. She often really dislikes them and is uncomfortable with them. She may admit this, or deny it, and try to disguise it, but if it is there, it is likely to come out in harsh, controlling ways. Teachers who have these feelings need help in understanding why they have them; they need help in altering them, and possibly even help in understanding that they should not be trying to teach young children.

The opposite of the teacher-tyrant is the submissive teacher relationship, one in which children are allowed to be demanding and controlling, and the teacher timorously accepts the domination of her children. Again, this is an extreme kind of teacher-child relationship, but it does occur, and it brings discomfort to everyone involved.

I am sure that children are very uncomfortable in this kind of role. It is even a little scary to know that *you,* a four-year-old, can control an adult, the teacher. Can you count on this person who seems so weak and ineffective? What if you really need help? Will she be able to stop you from doing dangerous things? Does she really care about you? These are some of the questions that the child may ask himself when the teacher-child relationship is of the quality I am describing.

The teacher end of this relationship is also an uneasy one. There is little joy in it, rather a fearful, timid, uncomfortable quality. She may wish she could be more assertive, but she doesn't dare to try, possibly because she is afraid she may fail. She is also the product of her own past experiences with teachers who may have been so repressive that she was determined not to follow in their footsteps or whose repressiveness left her scarred with a sense of her own unworthiness which lasted into her adulthood.

Teachers in this position can be helped to acquire more clarity, sureness, and warmth in their own relationships with children. It is helpful to discuss these feelings with an understanding consultant. The teacher who can learn to become more sure of herself, and can share her confidence with her children, will find that the resulting relationship is more satisfying to both herself and the children.

Both of the relationships which I have described are based on genuine feelings—one of superiority, the other of inferiority. Both lead to distortion and dissatisfaction in the teaching and learning process.

There is another kind of teacher-child relationship which is difficult to label except to call it artificial. It is based in uneasiness about "connecting emotionally" with children. It is expressed in a variety of ways. Sometimes it is expressed in sickly sweetness that seeks to disguise the underlying need to control and dominate. Children are addressed in endearing terms that are not genuinely felt. Children sense the falseness and are confused by it.

Another variety of the artificial relationship is the one in which the teacher tries to be child-like rather than teacher-like. This role is characterized by inappropriate playfulness on the part of the teacher. She may enter children's play, assuming dramatic roles assigned to her or chosen by her. She may engage in chasing games or active climbing or sliding on apparatus.

Her reason for assuming the role of another child is usually to cover up her own uncomfortableness with children, and to convince children that she enjoys them and feels at home with them. However, rather than reassuring children, such behavior is likely to confuse them. How should they respond to an adult who is not behaving like an adult? Some children are over-stimulated by this kind of un-teacher-like behavior. They exploit it in ways that are disturbing to the teacher as well as themselves. Exciting dramatic play involving jail, killing, injuring can get out of hand when the teacher allows herself to become involved as an active participant. She loses her identity as teacher, the person who can be depended upon, and she loses the control of the group, which the group needs her to maintain. A teacher who has permitted herself to be locked up in jail is hardly someone who can be counted upon to take care of you when you need her. And it is not easy for the teacher to switch roles from the incarcerated victim to the teacher person who is really in comfortable command of the situation.

There has been a vogue among some nursery schools of encouraging children to address teachers by their first names. The apparent reason for this is that such first-nameness tends to establish a relationship of comradeship, and a relaxed informal atmosphere. Those who do not approve of this mode of address have a hard time defending their position. They say that they prefer the more formal "Miss" or "Mrs." not merely as a sign of respect but rather as recognition that a teacher has a kind of adult authority and role that deserve the dignity of the official adult title. Since teachers beyond nursery school are usually addressed by the last name (except in certain avant-garde schools) it seems reasonable to begin the procedure at the nursery school level. It does not diminish or dilute a warm relationship between teacher and children to be called Miss Woodworth, instead of Sally. Nor should it make for a more cool, remote relationship. It chiefly makes Miss Woodworth seem a rather special person, a teacher. It is not primarily a matter of status recognition, but rather appropriate address.

Having described some of the negative teacher-child relationships that are obstacles to effective teaching and learning, I should like to try to describe a good relationship, an "emotional connection" that makes for mutual satisfaction and understanding between teacher and child.

Again we must start with the teacher and her feelings toward the children, and the "connections" she strives to make. First of all, she enjoys children and she feels good about being with them. She respects each child and his special uniqueness. She accepts each child, neither condemning or belittling his weaknesses, nor exaggerating his strengths. She lets the child know these feelings by her tone of voice, her facial expression and the words she speaks. She feels comfortable herself, feels confidence in her goal to help each child become his best self. She can admit her own limitations, can make mistakes and learn from them. She is alert in sensing each child's need of her, and responsive in trying to meet the need. She gives of herself willingly and freely. And all of this shines through the invitations to relate which she extends to her children. Her voice, her face, her movements and her actions reveal her feelings toward them, and invite responses of mutual respect and delight from which the good relationship develops.

Young children have an uncanny ability to sense the nature and quality of the relationship that any adult extends toward them, and they will respond accordingly. Overeager adults, in an effort to cover up their own uneasiness, will pounce upon children and bombard them with words, from which many children will quietly retreat. Some adults will try to capture the child by exhibitionistic tricks. A pediatrician observing in a nursery school once captivated a group of three-year-olds by making a mouse out of a handkerchief, and then making it disappear. His only other mode of communicating was to toss children over his head and between his legs. These performances were wildly exciting to the children, but limited in establishing any kind of dependable, trusting relationship. They also interfered with his own observations of the children.

The teacher who takes her cue from the child is more likely to be successful in establishing a relationship that is meaningful to both of them. She will accept the fact that she will be able to relate better with some children than with others. She will try to assess her own strengths and weaknesses, to track down the sources of her uneasiness that interfere with solid, comfortable relationships. She will be alert to children's responses and cues in helping her to know their needs.

The teacher needs to be the tone-setter of her classroom; she also needs to be the one who sets the relationship level. She needs to work toward establishing an emotional connection that is mutually friendly, respectful, clear, trusting, and caring. To the extent that she is successful in establishing these kinds of feelings, they will be reciprocated by her children, with a resulting relationship that will be a firm basis for effective and gratifying learning and teaching.

Working With Parents

Youthful as it is historically, the nursery school has made giant strides in its approach as well as its attitude toward the parents of the children it serves. In the past thirty years there has been a steady change in the attitude of teachers toward parents, and a corresponding change in the attitude of parents toward teachers: a change based on increased understanding and respect for each other.

In the early days of nursery education, parents were accepted but hardly welcomed by teachers. Parents were tolerated, and it was generally acknowledged that from time to time they might expect reports on the progress of their children. Teachers tended to blame parents for the child's shortcomings, and were annoyed when the parents did not accept the good advice which was so readily forthcoming from these seemingly all-knowing teachers. Parents were often intimidated by teachers who succeeded in making them feel that *only teachers* knew about children. If a child was hard to manage, the parents were blamed. Teachers expected to have to undo all the damage that had been done by the parents. Mothers were made to feel apologetic for the injuries they had wrought, and fathers might as well have been nonexistent.

One prominent nursery educator stated flatly that parent education should not be coupled with nursery education. She made it clear that parents would not be allowed to stay in the classroom, even on the first day of attendance. "We do not want the child to get the impression that school is for mothers, too . . . the child needs to know from the very start that the price of school fun is the separation from the mother." She adds that "if the parent cannot be won over, she should be ignored."

This extreme attitude of shutting out the parent was not echoed by other prominent preschool educators. Dorothy Baruch's classic book on nursery education is entitled *Parents and Children Go to School.*[4] She felt strongly that "without parents entering vitally into the picture, a nursery school is not a nursery school." She felt that parent education should not focus solely on the child, but should aim also at building confidence in parents. She felt that helping parents gain a greater measure of security in themselves as parents was more important than showering them with techniques for managing their children.

Before this enlightened point of view came into practice, parents were usually treated as people to be endured or to be taught. In those days, parents' meetings were strictly "telling" occasions. Parents were either told what they should do or not do, or were told what the teachers did and why it was right. The implication was "if you did the same, you would have no problems." They were told what toys to buy, what books to read. It seems quite likely that such practices succeeded admirably in increasing their sense of inadequacy.

Final reports to parents tended to be smug and preachy. They were full of documented evidence of progress on the part of the child, progress due to the excellent management of the teacher, of course. Final conferences, when they were held, were summaries of achievement and evidences of development, again as a result of school experiences. A parent's request for a conference was regarded with suspicion, as a challenge and somewhat of a threat.

This kind of behavior is understandable when one considers the historic role of the teacher. With a few notable exceptions, it has usually been a didactic one. The teacher has been known as the wise one, the teller. The parent has been another child to be told what to do.

If this looking backward seems somewhat rough on teachers,

it is partly in the interest of dramatizing the situation, and largely an indication of the lack of awareness among teachers that helping parents was part of their job. It has been pointed out that many of these early teachers were not so much smug as uninformed. Their fine training in "pure" child development rarely confronted them with the fact that the children they would teach would have parents, or that these parents would have feelings. Their seeming disregard of parents was based less on lack of caring or awareness than it was on their feelings of technical superiority.

Just as in the early days of our teaching we showed more concern about the physical child than about his psycho-social growth, so our concern with parents was primarily limited by physical boundaries, with little or no awareness of them as people from whom we could learn and with whom we could share. Our changing ways with parents are as much a sign of the growing up of the discipline of child development as they are the result of our own maturing as individual teachers.

All our well-meaning but limited gestures toward parents were done with honorable intentions, and were a reflection of the current set of "importances" of that era. Parents were impressed with the daily report of physical facts, and when these were first discontinued, some parents felt that somehow they were receiving less service.

However, there was an increasing awareness in the nursery school world that there was more to be shared than the mutual reporting of assorted physical facts of life. There was the growing feeling that parents had an important contribution to make to the teacher's understanding of the child, and that the nursery school had an obligation to share its knowledge of children with the parents. The past few years have witnessed increased concern for the development of this sharing. What to share and how to share it are now important parts of all good nursery school planning.

The whole picture changes when the shift to this base is made. The relationship between parents and teachers becomes one of mutual respect rather than suspicion. Such an approach assumes that teachers need to know something about individual family patterns, something of what life is like for this child in this family, and something of what life is like for these parents.

The teacher who approaches parents with this point of view realizes first that the parents of her group are as varied and individual as the children are. They are not just mothers and fathers; they are people, and each one is unique. The teacher notes that some parents are very young. These are the parents who married young and started having their family immediately. Other parents are older, either having married later or started their family later. Some parents are eager to learn and share their understanding and their questions. Some are aloof, hard to reach, critical. Some are enthusiastic, trusting, accepting. Some are confused, lacking in confidence.

Just as the teacher accepts the individuality of each child, she must accept each parent for himself. She does not blame him for being old or young, or critical or aloof. She does not feel superior to him. She tries to convey to each parent the feeling that she respects and values him. She also extends to him an invitation to share with her his understanding of his child. She welcomes the contributions which he may be able to make to the nursery school, whether it is playing the guitar, wielding a paint brush, or contributing to a discussion. And she also reveals the kinds of contribution which she, the teacher, can make to the parents.

From her observation and work with many children, she has acquired knowledge of the range of interests and skills of a particular age level that helps her to understand and accept each child. Parents who have known only one three-year-old can profit from the wider experience and knowledge of the teacher who has known hundreds of three-year-olds.

The teacher is equipped to help parents understand something of what to expect of their child, as well as some ways of managing the child. Many parents with the best intentions in the world approach young children with expectancies more suited to "middle-aged" children. Their demands are geared far beyond the child's ability to perform, and consequent disharmony between parent and child results. Some parents' expectations are geared too low, with the result that the child is permanently hitched to babyish standards with resulting anguish to both parents and the child, when the child attempts to bolt beyond the expectancies. Accordingly, the nursery school teacher has an important contribution to make to parents in extending their knowledge of the range of behavior that can be expected from young children, as well as some of the techniques of management that make for harmonious, meaningful living for the preschooler and his parents.

The teacher has another contribution to make to the parents: her knowledge of the activities that interest and delight young children; experiences that are meaningful and constitute opportunities for discovery as well as expression of learning. For many parents, the nursery school equipment itself is a source of enlightenment. They can observe the joy and satisfaction derived from blocks and boards and barrels, from water and dough and paint. Ingenious fathers have been inspired to reproduce some of the equipment with the result that back yards have become good places to play instead of sterile places where children are put and have to stay. Parents of nursery school children often become more discriminating purchasers of toys and books as a result of what they have learned from their observations in the nursery school.

In addition to clues about management and understanding behavior and providing for the child's play needs and interests, the teacher can convey to parents her understanding of the parent's own needs and goals. Too often, teachers in their eagerness to understand each child and to provide for his needs neglect to notice that the parent has some needs that merit consideration. Being a parent these days is not a simple task. Its demands are multiple and complex. Teachers can help by recognizing this fact, and sympathizing with the complexity of the job. Parents appreciate such understanding and support, and are likely to attack their problems fortified by the knowledge that they are not being criticized and blamed for their lack of perfection. This kind of understanding is an effective cement for better parent-teacher relationships.

What do the parents have to share with the teachers? First of all, they can share the "ingredients" of the child's life at home. It is helpful for teachers to have a picture of the family setting in which each child spends most of his hours. What constitutes the family? Large or small? New baby, or one coming? Who are the grownups? Are there helpers in the home? What about daddy? Is he rarely or frequently seen? What about space? Is it adequate, generous—or cramped? Has there been lots of moving or none? Are there other children to play with? What are the family expectations and standards with which this child must learn to cope? What do parents consider the assets and liabilities of this child? What do the parents expect from the school? These are some of the things that parents can share with teachers which will be mutually beneficial.

There is no neat set of rules or tidy formula for parents and teachers to follow in developing ways of sharing their particular knowledge and skills. However, over the years, some methods have proved more practical and rewarding than others. First there are the planned or formal occasions. Probably the most common method of communication is through conferences of parents with the teacher.

Most schools schedule an initial conference between the teacher and parents at the beginning of the school year, if possible before school starts. The chief purpose of such a meeting should be to provide an opportunity for getting acquainted. These conferences seem to be most successful when they are quite informal.

When the child and the mother together come for this first meeting, it can be a time of mutual learning and impression-receiving. The teacher may observe how the child enters the new situation, the quality of the relationship between the parent and the child. Does it seem to be one of casual confidence; is it warm and hearty; is it cool and critical; is it demanding or independent or dependent; is there evidence of strain or tension? Does the mother complain about the child or apologize for him? The teacher may learn a great deal about how the mother and child operate as a team without asking a question.

The teacher may ask about what kinds of things the child enjoys doing. She may ask if there are any particular concerns about the child that the mother wants her to be aware of. Does he tire easily? How about toileting; does he need reminding? She may give the mother a picture of the nursery school program, as well as procedures during the first few days; what to expect, what to look for.

It is well to remember that during this first visit the mother and child are receiving impressions of the teacher, just as she is learning about them. Is she friendly and welcoming? Is she patient and relaxed, or overeager and uneasy? Is she insistent and demanding? Does she wait for the child to approach her, or does she poke herself at the child? Does she talk too much?

During the school year, teachers and parents should feel free to call for conferences as they are needed. Some schools find it helpful to schedule regular conference times early in the school year, again at midyear and end of the year. Others have a more flexible plan. The important thing to remember is that conferences should be called not only for crisis occasions, but also for the unscheduled sharing of delights and discoveries which are mutually gratifying.

Sometimes brief, informal telephone reports are extremely welcome to both parents and teachers. The teacher who spontaneously calls the mother to report that John finally fingerpainted for the first time and enjoyed it tremendously is sharing her delight at the child's triumph and not just taking credit for it. The mother who calls to warn the teacher that excitement is high today because of an impending birthday party is helping the teacher and the child to adjust their gears to each other.

Home visits probably do more than any other contact to inform teachers about the quality of strain or lack of it under which the child and parents live. It helps the teacher to have a picture of the space in which the child spends most of his hours. Home visits also help parents to see the teacher as a person. And they are usually intoxicatingly joyous occasions for the children. There is something about seeing the teacher in the home that is so exciting and satisfying that the relationship is strengthened and cemented with comradeship and confidence.

Parent visits to the school are another important way of relating school and its ways to the parents and children. Not just observations on state or stated occasions, but spontaneous, unscheduled visits; visits not just for learning, but visits for enjoyment. These are the kind that communicate the spirit and the quality of the school experience. This can only happen, of course, when parents are made to feel genuinely welcome. Some schools schedule special "daddies' days" on holidays.

Group meetings are often the major scenes of parent-teacher sharing. Unless parents are included in the planning of such meetings, however, they tend to become one-way affairs, a kind of "we'll show you" demonstration.

There are many kinds of group meetings. Sometimes speakers may present material, either inspirational or informational. Question-answer meetings with a panel of assorted "experts" including parents and grandparents are often entertaining and challenging. Movies followed by discussion frequently open doors of thought to parents and teachers.

The chief hazard in depending solely on group meetings as a way of communicating with parents is that there tends to be too much reliance on talk and too little on thought. Parents and teachers need to evaluate these meetings to be sure that they do not become monotonously glorified "telling times."

Then there are all the informal ways of sharing with parents. Of these, the spontaneous telephone conversation mentioned before rates high, as well as the casual comments on arrival and departure. It is well for the teacher to remember that she is teaching when she least suspects it: by the way she greets children when they arrive, warmly or curtly or matter-of-factly; by the way in which she either ignores or shows pleasure and appreciation of their achievements. Parents note these things and learn from them.

There are many informal ways in which parents and teachers can learn from each other on occasions which are not primarily geared to *teaching* anything. Occasions which are purely social, such as nursery school family picnics, offer opportunities for sharing more than sandwiches. Good will and good fellowship are important ingredients of such affairs, and these are solid foundations on which to build confidence and respect.

Work-shop evenings or Saturdays when everyone turns out to repair or paint or mend result not only in improvement to the equipment but in improvement of human relations. Hammers and paint brushes become instruments for friendship as well as instruments for security and beautification.

Teachers can also contribute to the cementing of relationships between themselves and parents by showing interest in individual children on special occasions. Sending birthday cards or cheery notes when the child is ill not only impresses parents, but is evidence of the concern which the teacher feels for *their* child.

An alert teacher manages to include parents in her program planning. There may be a father who plays the guitar who could be invited to share his skill with the children. A mother who likes to sew might be lured into freshening up the doll corner. Fathers who are craftsmen or menders or builders have a big contribution to make. Parents who have special knowledge of birds or butterflies or airplanes can contribute insights and delight to group life. If there are such gifted parents and the teacher neglects to use their special skills, she is needlessly neglecting a whole area of curriculum enrichment, as well as missing an opportunity to communicate to parents the thought that she values them, and recognizes that they have something to contribute to the school. Such recognition and sharing is strong cement in building respect and understanding. In such a relationship the teacher is no longer a "teller"; she is a sharer.

There needs to be continuous exploring and evaluating of new ways of communication and understanding. However, whether the methods be formal or informal, organized or spontaneous, their success will depend on the sincerity of the teacher and her acceptance of the child and the parents as people whom she may possibly help, but from whom she may also learn.

Between teachers and parents there needs to be a mutuality of respect and valuing each other as people with jobs to do, with special skills, temperaments, feelings, and carings. On the part of teachers there needs to be less telling and more listening. There also needs to be the recognition and acceptance that not all parents will seem equally enthusiastic or even want to learn what we may think we have to teach. The teacher must recognize that parents as well as children have different levels of readiness to learn, and that these must be respected if our teaching is to be effective.

A sound parent-teacher relationship is measured by the quality of the relationship rather than by the number of successful meetings or conferences held during the year. Such a relationship involves a genuine sympathy and understanding of their separate and joint problems; an acceptance of one another without blame; a willingness to share knowledge and not just dictate it; a humility that admits that teachers don't know everything; and a real respect for the child, his parents, and their relationship. Add to these ingredients sprightliness and a sense of humor along with the sense of caring, and you are likely to have a relationship that is satisfying to the parents and the teacher. Teachers who have incorporated these qualities into their teaching role will never be heard to say to the somewhat apprehensive new mother who lingers on the first day of school, "Nursery school is for *children,* not for *mothers.*"

Children
Have Different Needs

A *place,* however perfectly planned and organized, and a *program,* however thoughtfully designed, would be empty indeed without *children* to make it come to life.

In the days preceding the opening of nursery school, the teacher is busily engaged in preparing the school rooms, filling them with materials that will interest and entice and challenge. Preparing the space for occupancy is an important preliminary, but suddenly the space seems empty in spite of its readiness, and the teacher is eager to see it filled with the children for whom it has been planned.

Who are the children? There will be fourteen to eighteen in each group: boys and girls aged three and four, with a range of backgrounds depending on the nature and purpose of the school. Strictly parochial schools are likely to select children from their particular religious affiliation, although some prefer a group representing a variety of religious backgrounds. Schools for the physically handicapped will select children with disabilities requiring the treatment which they are suited to provide. Day Care centers serve children from low income families where parents must work outside of the home. Therapeutic nursery schools serve children with emotional disturbances that need treatment. There are nursery schools that stress programs for intellectually gifted children. Nursery schools connected with colleges and universities serve as demonstration or laboratory schools for their students. These schools usually seek a cross section of children from families of various backgrounds. The Head Start programs are characterized by children from low-income "culturally deprived" families which qualify for the need.

Regardless of the nature of the school, each teacher of each group is confronted with an assortment of individual children for whom she has been preparing the place and the program. At first the group is merely a list of names. She may have a few facts about each child, his birthdate, his address, other siblings. But she needs to see him and begin to know him.

Some schools arrange to have children and parents come for a visit before school opens, as an introduction to the place and the teacher. When this is possible, the child has an opportunity to explore the classroom and the materials in it. He finds his locker and claims it. He gets a feeling that this is his place, and that the teacher is his friend. The teacher also gains an impression of each child without the distraction of other children.

Sometimes home visits by the teacher before school opens aid in the process of introduction. For some children, to see the teacher on their home ground makes the teacher less strange and formidable.

The teacher who greets her children has all her antennae alerted to receive the unique individual signals of each child. She expects them to be different. She sharpens her awareness of their individual differences and her observation of them.

What does she see when a child first enters her classroom? Her first impression is likely to be of the physical appearance of the child. Let's observe her observation of a new child entering for the first time. Joel is the child. He is just four. Even before she greets him, she may notice that he seems solid, somewhat chunky; round faced, solemn expression. He stands inside the door with his mother. The teacher smiles as she greets him and his mother. "Hi, Joel! and Mrs. Barker. I've been expecting you. I'm glad you came to see your new school. I'm your teacher, Miss Bailey. Would you like to look around and see what we have in this school?"

Miss Bailey will be interested to observe Joel's response to her welcome. Will he cling to mother and turn away and hide his face? Will he grin a silent response? Will he ignore her greeting and start exploring the place and the things in it? Will he pull his mother along with him, or abandon her?

If he moves, what is the nature of his movements? Are they swift and sure or slow, sluggish or precise? Does he cover all the space in flitting movements, or settle into one area and stay? Does he seem well coordinated or clumsy, loose or tight?

What about his facial expression? Is it animated, sparkling with pleasure and excitement; or is it grim, gloomy, suspicious, or angry? Is it impassive, masklike, or seemingly apprehensive?

What about his language and the quality of his speech? Is his speech clear or unclear? Does he chatter freely and meaningfully? Does he demand attention by intrusive talking or questioning? Or is he silent?

What choices does he make in the room? Having surveyed the room and its contents does he seem to make a selection and stay with it, or does he sample and abandon a number of materials? Does he look but not touch? Does he ask for help from his mother or the teacher, or does he plunge into materials independently? Does he show signs of testing the limits of the situation by throwing blocks or splattering paint or tossing books or puzzles?

By observing Joel closely but casually during this first visit, Miss Bailey will assemble a few clues about what kind of little person he seems to be, the use he will make of the nursery school, and the ways in which she may help him. She realizes that this is a very skimpy capsule first impression, but she stores it away in her mind or in a brief written report that will become part of Joel's record in the nursery school.

She will be interested to check her first impression with subsequent impressions when other children are present. Nursery schools often plan the early days to be short sessions with only half the group attending at one time. This enables the teacher to get a clearer impression of each child, and also enables each child to have more of the teacher's attention than would be possible if the whole group were present.

The teacher will continue to observe the child's entrance into the playroom; the extent to which he needs or demands his mother's presence; the extent to which he seeks the help or attention of the teacher; the consistency of his choices of activity and his patterns of movement and communication. She will also notice his response to the other children. Does he ignore them? Is he selective, choosing one child or excluding certain children? Is he contagiously explosive, seeking attention through behavior that annoys or disturbs? Is he clownish, seeking to attract attention by silly behavior? Is he cautious about approaching other children? Is he demanding, bossy, bullying? Is he impulsive, eager but bumbling, spontaneous, friendly, shy, cautious, devious, passive?

The teacher watches his relationships with other children, and without labeling them, tries to understand his strengths and needs so that she can formulate a plan toward helping him.

The child who gets into trouble with himself and with others makes major demands on the teacher's attention and energy. In her endeavor to meet the needs of these over-demanders and disrupters, she frequently loses sight of the under-demanders, the quiet accepters. Such children can be neglected and miss out on the positive teaching they deserve but do not demand. It is important that from time to time teachers assess the ratio of teaching attention they give to these two kinds of children. It is not fair to short cut the "good little citizen" in his share of teaching time in favor of the disturbed and disturbing child who demands and usurps large portions of teacher time and energy.

The teacher will also be interested in observing the extent to which her initial impression of the child's response to her is sustained or altered when other children enter the group. She will be aware that some children will seem to maintain their independence of her, while others will need her presence and her reassurance. Some will be casual, seeking her only when they need her help. Some will demand her attention and actively seek her approval. Some may cling; others ignore. Some will welcome her authority; others will challenge and defy it: "You are not the boss of me!" To some she will need to be something of a mother at moments of stress. Her hope is that eventually she will become a friend to all her children, a person whose goal it is to help each child to become his very best self.

She begins by accepting each child for himself. She welcomes his unique style and flavor. She respects his individual design of movement, communication, action, thought. She steers him in the direction of the best utilization of his talents. She does not attempt to change him into a different kind of person but she may attempt to alter his special individual pattern when it is an obstacle to harmonious development. She will not attempt to make the aggressive child into a passive child, but she will work hard to direct his aggression into constructive channels. She will work to help the passive child to dare to reach out and assert himself. She will try to offer appropriate challenges to all her children. She will be alerted to and rejoice in their differences.

At the end of the day she will take time to think about the ways in which each of her children revealed himself. Which were the children whose voices echo in her ears, talking, chattering, laughing, crying—the easy verbal communicators. Which was the child whose voice she had not heard at all? Which was the child who could not be parted from the guinea pig? Who was the child who seemed hypnotized, if not immersed, in waterplay? Which was the child enchanted by books, reluctant to leave them? Who was the boss and manager of the doll corner, chiefly occupied in keeping others out of it? Which ones were the tasters and flitters, who could not become involved in anything for long? Who were the watchers?

These were her children, each one revealing to his teacher something of himself, his skills, his interests, his feelings, his needs, not always in words, but through the language of his behavior. And she, his teacher, must be constantly tuned to receive his signals and to respond to them in ways that will help him to be his best self. Yes, children are different, and she rejoices in their differences. They have different needs; it is a challenge to her to discover them, and to try to meet them in her teaching.

The Over-Aggressive Child

The hyperactive, aggressive child is always a challenge to the teacher. He is often difficult to manage in the group. He frequently frightens and disturbs other children. His behavior, which is usually rough-and-tumble and attacking, has an explosive quality that is often contagious.

The teacher of this kind of child is confronted with multiple challenges both in understanding and management. First, she needs to learn something of the home environment and of the child's developmental history. What are the pressures and expectations for behavior that are being exerted upon him? What is his position in the family? Is he difficult to manage at home? Has he always been a "fighter?" What was he like as a baby?

She will not blame him for being aggressive, she will endeavor to discover and understand the source of his aggressiveness, and she will try to help him to direct it into constructive, rather than destructive channels.

This is not an easy task, and the teacher with one or more of these super-charged children in her group will find that it takes all of her ingenuity and patience to keep them from disrupting the group. But her goal is larger than that. She aims also at helping the child himself to build in controls that will keep him from disturbing the peace. This involves a long range program. It is not achieved in a day or two.

I should like to describe a child who presented these challenges to the teacher from the first day he entered school. I shall call him Peter. I shall describe him through the eyes of his teacher and excerpts from written records she accumulated during his two years at nursery school. These records provided a vivid source of material that helped her to be aware of the nature of his problem as well as the direction of his development.

The nature of these notes varied from occasional "spot" records, written at the moment of the action, to end-of-the-morning recollections of certain incidents she wished to remember. There were also midyear and end-of-year summaries of behavior, and notes of parent conferences.

This description of Peter culled from her notes will be necessarily a condensed one, utilizing dramatic highlights to show the quality of his behavior, the ways in which his teacher tried to help him, and the gains he made in self-understanding and self-control. The reader needs to remember that this is a capsule presentation of two long years of living and learning. The changes that occurred were not achieved by magic, but by hard work on the part of the teacher, his parents, and Peter himself.

His teacher describes him as a very attractive young three-year-old, sturdy, well-proportioned, with a shining face that could beam with delight, that could laugh with nose-wrinkling charm, but could also assume a glazed expression with a tense mouth and a staring blank look.

His movements were quick, but scattered, particularly his leg movements. His run was characterized by loose gangling leg work and over-all uncoordinated movements of arms and torso. He seemed to have difficulty pulling his feet off the ground.

His energy level was high and explosive. He attacked materials with vigor and abandon. He would wham an inset puzzle on the table, scattering the pieces, but would proceed to assemble it hastily and with intensity. Upon completion, he would throw it aside.

He showed little interest in paints except for aggressive brush strokes that seemed primarily an attack on the paper. Crayons were used in the same vigorous manner without apparent interest in color or pattern.

Blocks, trains, and trucks interested him, although too often he used them as instruments of attack and destruction. To knock down a building had more appeal than to construct one. And trucks and trains were engines of attack rather than purveyors of goods or people. Clay was for pounding—"the flattest pancake in the world." Sand was for digging deep. It was also for throwing, particularly at people. Carpentry was an opportunity to pound and saw with vigor, rather than for construction.

Peter was a surprisingly good story listener. He was alert and attentive, responsive to the mood of the story, and a good contributor to it. His language was effervescent, bubbling and clear in spite of his consistent substitution of "f" or "v" for "th."

He had a large vocabulary and a highly imaginative, frequently poetic use of language. One spring day he asked the teacher, "Which do you like ve best, Miss B., a fistle or a forsifia?"

He was a hearty but somewhat off-key singer at music times. Rhythms excited him, and he usually became wild and uncontrolled, running around, bumping into furniture and other children.

It was in relation to other children that he had his greatest difficulties. He was a ruthless attacker. He was a hair-puller, a lightning biter, a pusher, a kicker, scratcher, and hitter. His attacks were usually unprovoked. A little girl sitting quietly in a packing case would be the victim of his snatching fingers, emerging tearfully while Peter clutched a handful of her blond hair.

A visiting baby, sitting on its mother's lap, was suddenly swooped upon. Peter seized the tiny hand and bit the finger deeply. While the startled baby was being comforted and Peter was being confronted with his deed, he asked, "Did it (the bite) go fru to ve uvver side? Did it bleeve?"

The teacher describes Peter as a child of dramatic contrasts, characterized by vigor in everything. He had tremendous drive, galloping energy, and directness. He had a swooping quality of engulfing life whether it was blocks or babies or someone's blond hair.

In the early days, there were periods of frenzied weeping at the slightest frustration. These diminished and he was able to announce upon arrival, "I would like to stay in vis school till I go to a office." There would be days when he would snatch and tear and destroy the magnolia blossoms in the school garden, and another day when he would reminisce plaintively, "Remember when we went on ve hike and found ve pussy pillows? Vey were so soft."

The flashing contrast of extremes of response were revealed in many ways. There was his early insistent and anxious dependence on ritual and routine: "Do vis button first!" and to his mother, "Kiss me ve *right* way!" This contrasted with the later casual pleasure he took in routine. "It don't matter, do it?"

More dramatic were the changes in social techniques from a roistering, violent instantaneous attack upon the slightest or no provocation to a plaintive, wistful, "Oh, my, I need a shovel; could I spare your shovel, John?"

His teacher describes the tone of one of his shinier days. Peter was bursting with joie de vivre. His body seemed unable to keep up with his bouncing spirits. He was sportive, joyous, scattered, affable. He noticed the remains of yesterday's fray with John, "Vat's where I hit you in ve eye, remember, John? Boy, vat hurt, din't it? And you cried, din you? And we certainly hit, hit, hit, and punch, punch, din we? Boy, oh, boy!"

Another day she wrote, "An unseen beginning of a battle with Larry. It was being silently waged with Peter definitely on the victorious side, until I rescued Larry, bleeding and weeping, deep scratches close to his eye and on mouth and forehead. There were frequent sudden forays with Robert, bopping head with boards."

On still another day, she describes fire engine play with John. "He was easily and intermittently distracted by John's deliberate and appealing nonsense sounds and rhythmic gestures. There was much chanting of 'Boy, gee, me!' and 'God Murphy!' He announced he was going to be a fireman until he went to Sunday School. Out of doors he ate pecks of snow, said his hands were 'cold as dead!' As he was getting dressed to go home he announced, 'I'm going to be speedy as a squirrel.' He dashed off, returned and said, 'I used to be slow as a turtle, but now I'm speedy as a squirrel; how speedy is a squirrel, Miss B.?' He was off again to hunt for a mitten and on returning said, 'I guess I'm *medium* speedy; vat's pretty speedy, isn't it, Miss B.?' "

During the two years that Peter was in the nursery school, some important changes took place. He was not made over into a different person. He continued to be easily frustrated, and to respond with instantaneous and explosive hostility. But the occasions were rarer, and he was better able to control his violent impulses. Both frequency and degree of aggressive attacks diminished. He was capable of sustaining longer, more concentrated periods of attention to constructive activities. His joys were shinier, his jokes funnier, his peace deeper. There was evidence of occasional serenity and the belief that life is not all threat. There was also evidence of the acceptance of the fact that certain consequences follow certain behavior, without judgments being brought against him.

Peter had had the opportunity of being in a place where he could be himself without being condemned for his shortcomings. He was also helped to substitute more acceptable modes of behavior. He was helped to learn that bad impulses are not irretrievably evil, and that you can be helped to do something about them.

These changes did not occur by magic. They came about slowly with the help of the teacher, who mobilized all of her insights, understanding, and caring, and energy to do the job.

Through conferences with Peter's mother, she learned that Peter had always been active and aggressive. His aggressiveness was stimulated by a home situation that imposed strains on him. Peter had been born somewhat late in the lives of his parents. They admitted that they knew little about what to expect of young children, and that they had probably imposed high and harsh standards which were inappropriate and against which he rebelled. Both parents worked and Peter was at home with two ailing grandparents and an older housekeeper who alternately teased and scolded him. The house was small; space for an active child was cramped. His parents were greeted each evening with a rehearsal of his bad deeds of the day. Life was not easy for Peter, and he chose to fight out against it.

The teacher was able to help the parents to understand the difficulties of the situation for Peter and to think of ways of easing it. Arrangements were made for occasional visits with other children. Suggestions were made for some outdoor play equipment that would be fun for Peter and also drain off some of his energy. It was also suggested that Peter have some space in the house that would be his, to which he could retreat, where he would be safe from nagging grownups. A little time with Daddy in the evening for reporting not just the day's misdeeds, but the day's delights and discoveries, was suggested.

The parents were grateful and tried hard to alter the restricted, harsh regime to which Peter had been subjected. They were relieved that the teacher did not seem to blame them, nor did she label Peter a pre-delinquent. She admitted that he had a hard time managing his energy and that he got into trouble with other children.

In nursery school, the major problem was that of channeling Peter's explosive aggressiveness into acceptable constructive behavior. The teacher began by making it clear to Peter that she was going to try to help him, not just stop him. She greeted him warmly each day, with the hope and expectation that it would be a good day for him. She made an effort to steer him in the direction of an activity that would capture his interest and absorb his attention. She would point out new materials that might appeal to him; or she might remind him of an unfinished task that he had begun the previous day and had wanted to complete. She knew that he needed help in starting his day, and that a good start was the best possible insurance that his day would continue to be satisfying.

Peter's teacher had also learned that transition times—shifts from one activity to another—were difficult for Peter to manage. Accordingly, she was alert to his need for help at these times. She would warn him about impending changes, "It's almost time to put away the tools," or "In a few more minutes, we need to get ready for juice," or "I'll help you clean up the clay table so we'll be ready for juice."

At all times she endeavored to make it clear to Peter that there were some things that were not permitted in the nursery school classroom or playground. There were rules that every child needed to learn about and to respect. These rules or limits were not coercive or randomly selected. They were reasonable and consistent safeguards for group and individual welfare. "Blocks are for building, not for throwing or hitting." "Tools must be used at the workbench." "Food is for eating, not for messing." "Children don't like to have their buildings or paintings or possessions destroyed." These and similar rules aimed at respecting the rights of others as well as the intrinsic nature and function of materials were applicable to all the children, not just Peter. But they were harder for Peter to accept and remember. His destructive, aggressive impulses were so intense that it was difficult for him to apply the brakes that would keep him within the boundaries of the limits.

The teacher's role in helping Peter was to state the limits clearly and, when possible, to anticipate and prevent their being shattered by Peter's impetuous need. She soon learned to sense a rising tension in Peter, as well as to be aware of situations that set him off on destructive binges. She helped him to recognize these signals and situations, and helped him to move out of them before exploding. When Peter was one of many children block-building in one area, she would point out the hazards and help him relocate in a less congested area.

She was also alert to his need for vigorous action, and she searched for legitimate avenues for his aggressive needs. She provided clay that could be pounded flat, wood for sawing and hammering with nails, a punching bag to punch. "I have a hundred and fifty steam!" he announced one day as he pummeled the bag instead of another child's head. She provided a football for kicking, a digging place for deep digging, rakes to rake the leaves into piles for tumbling and throwing, tumbling mats for somersaults and tricks, space to run in, activities that would consume some of the "one hundred fifty steam" without disturbing or injuring other children. One of his favorite activities was pounding and hacking wooden orange crates into pieces that could then be used for kindling.

All of these activities had the virtue of both being joyous as well as high energy consumers. Many of them produced constructive results as well as draining off aggressive energy. Two boards nailed together with vigorous hammering, after having been equally vigorously sawed, could become an airplane or a boat. Fist-flattened clay could become the "flattest pancake in the world." And even the splintered orange crates could be stacked as kindling for fireplace burning.

Peter's teacher was not only a clarifier of rules and an appropriate limit setter and channeler of aggressive energy. She was quick to point out his successes, and to approve of behavior which she was trying to encourage. "Good for you, Peter! Your truck carried all those loads of blocks to your airport, and it didn't bump into a single building!" Or, "you really remembered about not pushing children on the high, rocky place, didn't you?" Or reminiscing about the "olden days" when it used to be hard for him to control his aggressive impulses. "Remember when you used to snatch Jimmy's shovel when you wanted one, and now you've learned to ask for it instead of grabbing! That must make you feel so good, and it certainly makes Jimmy feel good! It makes *me* feel good, too!" These expressions of genuine approval had a very positive effect on Peter. He became increasingly aware of the fact that his teacher was trying to help him and that her pleasure in his successes was not just that he had pleased her, but that he had learned things that made him feel good, too. He himself was able to reminisce toward the end of his second year in nursery school, "Remember when I was li'l, Miss B.? Remember when I din understand?"

In all of this, Peter's teacher was trying to help him to acquire a different portrait of himself from the one which he had brought to the nursery school. This involved more than a mere shift of "labels" from bad to good. It involved a real shift in "image," from "I'm the kind of person who grabs and snatches, knocks down, hits, bites, destroys" to "I'm the kind of person who can accept limits, who will respect the rights of others, who will share, who can enjoy without destroying."

Peter's teacher never doubted that he could learn. There were days when she felt discouraged, and days when her confidence was challenged. There were days when she needed to remove Peter from the group to terminate the destructive rampage, not for punishment, but because in those states, he could not manage to be a member of the group. He was not banished in disgrace, but removed to spare him from his own inability to control his aggressive impulses. "It's too hard for you to be with other children right now. You can play here by yourself for awhile. You may come back when you really feel you would like to be with the other children and that you can manage it."

But even in these moments of stress, she did not feel that Peter was hopeless. She recognized that he needed help in accepting the consequences of his aggressive behavior; that other children would retaliate in kind, or choose not to play with him, or that he would be temporarily denied the pleasure of their company. She never condemned him. She strove patiently and continuously to give him a feeling of being so valued that he would want to be his best self, the self that she felt so sure was there.

Peter was not an easy child to have in a group. His demands on the teacher were intense and consuming. They strained her patience, her ingenuity and her energy, but never her faith. She maintained a steady confidence in his ability to become a "good little citizen," and a contributing, rather than a destructive member of the group. And he did!

She describes two incidents that occurred in the spring of his second year in nursery school, as evidence of the gains he had made in controls and understanding.

He had been building a complicated tower-like construction of blocks when Joe, hauling a truck load of blocks, bumped into the tower and demolished it. Before the teacher could get to the demolition site to save Joe's life, Peter had turned to him and asked, "Was vat a accident?" Joe nodded, "Yes." "OK, if it was a accident, I'll play wiv you. Could you help me build it up again?"

Another time, Peter had gathered all the interlocking trains to himself. Mike was longing to have some but didn't quite dare to ask for them. The teacher interceded with the comment, "You know, Peter, it doesn't seem quite fair for you to have *all* the trains when Mike has none and would really like some. What do you think we could do about it?"

"Bevide vem, vat's what!" was Peter's answer. He proceeded to divide them equally between himself and Mike. When he had finished, he said, "Ver, do you fink vat's fair?"

It was indeed fair, but it was also evidence of how much Peter had learned about managing his own acquisitive and aggressive impulses. He had learned it from his teacher's unwavering confidence that he *could* learn.

Peter's teacher continued to see him from time to time during his elementary school years and had occasional reports from his mother. He was a good student in school, eager to learn, responsive and accepting of reasonable rules. He continued to be excitable and intense, but was not a major disrupter of peace or challenger of authority. He did well in college. His teacher likes to feel that his preschool experiences contributed to his success. Without the understanding and positive guidance during those early years, his overly aggressive impulses might easily have become fixed, and prevented him from becoming the constructive citizen which he became. Even his choice of a profession seemed to echo the efforts of his teacher in trying to help him to direct his destructive impulses into positive directions. He chose a career in surgery, where he seems to be happy and successful.

The Passive,
Non-Assertive Child

The behavior of the overaggressive child demands the attention of the teacher. Not only is her attention captured, but her energies are summoned into action. She must be constantly alert to prevent explosions, or to divert them in a harmless direction. She must also try to determine the causes which sparked the explosions. She must deal with the child as well as protect other children and materials from damaging attacks. This kind of child is understandably a major consumer of teacher attention, thought, and action.

By contrast, the passive, nonassertive, shy child is frequently by-passed. His behavior does not attract anyone's attention. It is often a relief to a teacher to have a child like this in the group. Since his apparent needs are so modestly expressed, she is enabled to direct more of her energy and attention to the more boisterous demands of the aggressive children.

However, these passive children deserve the same degree of attention and concern from the teacher as the more vigorous action children who are proclaiming their needs with words and muscles. The passive child's needs for understanding and guidance are no less real because they are less visible or audible. Often these children are suffering deeply from their lack of expressiveness. Their silence and passivity are quiet but strong signals for help. David was one of these children who could

have been by-passed. Fortunately he was not. His teacher was immediately drawn to this solemn-faced little old man of a child. She watched him closely during his first mornings at the nursery school. His movements were slow, his face solemn and unresponsive. He was silent. He watched other children but made no effort to communicate with them.

On the first morning he pushed a wheelbarrow around the yard, watching the block-building of two little girls. When they left their construction, he stolidly barged into the building, knocking down the walls with quiet effectiveness. He showed no evidence of either hostility or pleasurable excitement in the action. He pushed all the boards into a jumble, walked over them with an impassive expression, almost as if he were unaware of what he was doing. And yet the teacher sensed a quality of definiteness and determination about the action. She wondered if he would have dared to do it while the girls were actively engaged in the construction project. Apparently the quiet destruction had not disturbed the children who had abandoned the building, and the teacher decided not to confront David with his action at this time. But she did not forget it. She stored it away in her mind and in her notebook for future reference.

David was the only child in the group who refused the mid-morning snack of crackers and juice. He said nothing but refused to sit down at the table, wandered around the edges of the room, watching the other children in a somewhat furtive manner. When asked if he needed to go to the bathroom, he shook his head and continued to pace the room, occasionally picking up a toy, then dropping it.

During the morning he showed no animation, and no evidence of either enjoyment or distress. His mother hovered about uneasily, seeming to anticipate that he would be disturbed if she left. He stayed in her general vicinity, but made no effort to contact her and certainly did not cling to her. When she finally left, he showed no evidence of concern or anxiety, nor did he show any special pleasure in her return. He merely glanced in her direction, then looked away. When it was time to go home, she took his hands, and he pulled away from her with a gesture of unwillingness to leave.

The teacher came to the aid of his mother, said goodbye to

both of them, said she was glad they had come and that she would see them tomorrow.

She sensed that David was a child whose passivity very likely cloaked a considerable amount of suppressed hostility. It was evident that he possessed few social techniques that he could make use of. She recalled her impression of the mother when she had come for the registration interview. Mrs. Manning seemed gentle, unaggressive, cautious, almost apologetic. She had said very little about David, except that he had no children to play with, and she was eager for him to have the companionship of other children. She was obviously inspecting the school situation, and revealing little about herself or David. She admired the physical set-up of the school.

In later conferences, Mrs. Manning was freer to talk about some of her concerns about David. She said he had never been a very active child. His father had recently purchased some climbing apparatus, a slide and swing for their yard. David hadn't attempted to use it, much to Mr. Manning's disappointment. He seemed more interested in small toys, cars and airplanes. He could identify many kinds of cars, and was interested in distinguishing varieties of work trucks and their functions. She said that he had never talked "baby talk," that he had a surprising vocabulary and used long words correctly.

She was concerned about his shyness and lack of social graces. When other children came to visit, he ignored them or quietly but firmly prevented them from using his toys. He was never able to greet neighbors or friends who came to the house, nor could he respond to their greetings, and this distressed her.

She described him as having been an easy baby except for early refusal of food which had persisted. He also tended to be constipated, and this was a worry to her. There had been no particular difficulty in toilet training, except for resistance to sitting on the toilet when he was constipated.

She said it seemed hard for him to accept punishment or scolding, and that she was often at a loss as to how to manage him. She described the younger brother as a much more relaxed child whom David tended to tease and try to upset. "He gets wound up when he plays with Jamie, runs around, snatches his toys, pushes him over, until Jamie rebels with shrieks. When

I tell him to stop bothering Jamie, he says, 'But I love Jamie and I love this house, and I love my room and all the things in it, and I don't like to have you be cross with me.'"

Mrs. Manning was clearly eager for help in understanding and managing David. The teacher felt that she would be co-operative and glad to accept whatever insights and assistance the nursery school might be able to offer. She seemed genuinely eager to do what was right, but was obviously not sure about what this was for David.

As the teacher continued to observe David in the nursery school, she began to assemble clues that gave her a picture of David's interests, skills, problems, and needs. She watched him with other children. She noticed his reserve, his lack of spontaneous rapport. He seldom sought out other children, and he usually resisted children who tried to contact him. He spent a long time watching the other children. This was not desultory watching. He seemed to be soaking in impressions of what they were doing. He made no advances toward them, and tended to retreat from their advances. Occasionally he would silently and cautiously approach another child with a teasing gesture of tossing a toy in his direction.

As the year progressed, he became ingenious in inventing ways of relating to other children. He would build a store with blocks, and "sell" rugs or blankets or groceries. The children accepted this role and frequently consulted him about what his store was selling today. His "business" was usually conducted silently, but efficiently.

Increasingly he was included in family dramatic play, usually choosing the role of "big brother," which he seemed to enjoy in a quiet kind of way.

As he began to feel more at ease with the other children, he became less furtively aggressive. Rather than slyly snitching and hoarding pails and shovels in the sandbox, he would openly snatch what he wanted.

One day while getting dressed to go outdoors, he slapped Alan's face with his leather glove. Alan objected and said he didn't like it. The student teacher commented that it probably hadn't felt very good; then she asked David why he had felt like doing it.

David: "I don't know why."

Teacher: "Is it because you don't like Alan?"

David: (Nodding head affirmatively) "Yes."

Teacher: "You *don't* like Alan?"

David: "No, I don't like most people."

Teacher: "Do you like Joel?"

David: (Looking uncertain) "I don't know."

Teacher: "Do you like Debby?"

David: "I don't know."

Teacher: "Do you like Barby?"

David: "I don't know."

Teacher: "Do you like Jamie?" (His brother)

David: (Smiling, eyes lighting) "Yes."

Teacher: "Your mommy and daddy?"

David: "Yes!"

Teacher: "Me?"

David: (Clouding again) "I don't know."

Teacher: "Is it because you don't know us very well?"

David: (Brightening and seemingly relieved) "Yes, yes, that's right."

Teacher: "Perhaps when you know us better, you will know whether you like us or not."

David: "Ummmmmm."

David's teacher noted that there was steady progress in his ability to relate to other children during the course of the school year. He progressed from watching and surreptitious, sly teasing to occasional decisive attacks. When directly frustrated or attacked by other children, he retaliated with puppy-like battling gestures, or with silent scratches and kicks. When children refused to accept him in dramatic play, he left the scene, seeming to ignore the situation. The teacher suspected that he was longing to join the play, but lacked the techniques that would permit him to join it. He never became a bouncy life-of-the-party child. He never became an outstanding leader. He sustained his loner role, but he advanced in his ability to seek companionship, and even to initiate dramatic play. For several weeks in the spring, he was "the father" in the family play. He selected his family and with quiet authority designated appropriate roles to the others.

David: "Betsy could be the baby. Jill will be the mother. Nancy will be the cousin. The mother has to go to the super-market to buy the groceries. Who will be the baby-sitter? OK, Joe, you be. And the father has to go to his office to design a bridge, because he's that kind of an engineer."

This, from David, who had started his nursery school ex-perience with sly glances and negative head shaking as his only communication tools!

His relationships with the adults in the school followed a similar pattern of initial caution, almost suspicion, gradually moving toward trust and acceptance. In the early days, he main-tained a passive resistance, refusing to respond to suggestions. He remained cool and aloof, ignoring even friendly advances.

But he made progress in daring to relate to adults as well as to children. There was a noticeable increase in his "at-easeness" with them. He frequently engaged in conversation, some of which he initiated. He seemed eager to share his ideas about his build-ings. He revealed apparent satisfaction and even pleasure in a moderate display of affection. He seemed to enjoy the teacher's arm around his shoulder. He leaned against her while she read a story. He could take but not give a hug. He even told his mother that he liked his teacher, that she was his friend. And one day he nearly laughed out loud as he told her a joke. "Hey, Miss Gay, did you know that peaches are growing on the apple tree?"

His response to routines which were largely teacher dictated followed a similar pattern of initial resistance, followed by cau-tious acceptance, and eventual moderate enjoyment.

In a midyear report to his parents, his teacher indicated that there had been a marked change in his attitude toward the routines of the nursery school day. Early in the year he tended to ignore, avoid, resist, or slither out of them. Putting away toys, getting ready for lunch, either bored or annoyed him. He re-fused to participate in the juice and cracker snack. He made no effort to cooperate in putting on outdoor clothing. He seemed helpless about managing the mechanics of buttons and straps. He stood, a listless statue, waiting for the teacher to help him. Toileting was a private affair. After the teacher had helped with the clothing, David would dismiss her. "You wait outside."

During the year, there was a noticeable relaxing of resistance in all of these routines. He accepted the "putting away" procedures matter-of-factly, and progressed from a slow motion kind of token response to assuming his share of the job with alacrity and apparent satisfaction and pride.

He continued to resist the juice routine intermittently to the end of the year. No pressure was ever put on his participating. Sometimes he drank the juice; sometimes he refused it. The teacher felt that he came to enjoy it, but continued to hold out against conforming as a way of challenging the adult.

He developed more skill in managing his clothing, putting on snowsuit and boots. He made efforts to master buttons and zippers, but never seemed particularly interested in the process.

Toileting became a less self-conscious affair. He was able to go to the bathroom without insisting that the adults or other children leave the room. The whole procedure seemed to acquire a casual quality that matched the general loosening of obstinant resistance and aloofness.

This "loosening" was also evident in his use of his body. His tight, stiff little statue-like stance changed to a somewhat more relaxed and casual pose. His running was tight; his shoulders stiff and tied. There was little apparent pleasure to him in running, but at least he ran.

His teacher describes him as the "least climbing child in the group." He was persistent in refusing to climb the horizontal ladder, or the apple tree. When encouraged to climb the ladder, he would respond firmly and flatly, "I don't want to!" He explained his reluctance to climb the apple tree by announcing, "I don't want to hurt the apples." He was willing to climb on packing cases, and seemed to enjoy scrambling over the rocks, which he managed to do with moderate skill and apparent satisfaction. He also seemed to enjoy hauling loads of blocks and building materials in wagons.

The music teacher reported that at first during the music period he seemed dazed. He chose to sit in a chair, watching, or kicking other chairs. He refused to participate in the action games and rhythms. He would stand in the middle of the floor with children revolving around him. When children were relaxing on the floor, he would slyly push at them with his feet.

Eventually he began to participate in a half-hearted, self-conscious, almost furtive fashion. She described his movements as "unbuoyant and stiff," but revealing some evidence of a sense of time. By spring, a student teacher reported that he had been very active in a music session, as long as she held his hand. He ran freely, pulling her. Afterwards, when going to the playground, she commented to David that he seemed to have had fun during music. David smiled, then giggled, "Yes, I did have fun. Sometimes I don't do anything. I don't know why."

Student: "Well, probably some days you feel like doing something, and some days you don't."

David: (Smiling) "Yes, I guess that's it. Sometimes it's monotonous. (Pause) And I know what that means—the same old thing."

David's mother had reported with some pride that his vocabulary was large and that he used big words like "magnificent," "indigestible," and "surreptitious." Once when his teacher had visited his home, he took her to show her his room. It was richly stocked with expensive toys. She admired his collection of trucks. His response to her comment was: "Anyway, I know lots of hard words."

He probably did know lots of hard words, but it seemed a somewhat pathetic accomplishment for a four-year-old. His vocabulary may have been large, but his verbal communication was meager. However, it, too, became freer. He even began to be able to express his feelings in words.

One day he said to his teacher in a tone combining uneasiness with indignation, "You know what somebody once said to me?"

Teacher: "What?"

David: "Somebody said he'd saw my head off—and then he didn't."

This was accompanied by a tiny smile and frown, as if it had been a relief that the threat had not been carried out.

Teacher: "Don't you think he was joking or teasing you?"

David: "I guess he might have been."

The teacher was pleased that he could now verbalize his worries, instead of silently carrying them around with him.

He listened with rapt attention to stories, and often made intelligent and pertinent contributions to group discussions.

During the story time, he sat stiffly with a solemn professional air of "no nonsense." He preferred stories with informational content.

Along with freer speech, freer body movements, more ease in relation to children and adults, there was a steady increase in confidence and enjoyment in using the play materials. His paintings progressed from cautious, rigid, careful strokes of stripes or concentric circles, to vigorously scrubbed colors, one on top of each other. These were not as attractive to the viewer, but they revealed a loosening up of David's muscles, and a moving away from tightness and constriction to more freedom and enjoyment.

He enjoyed crayoning. He had definite color preferences, announcing that purple was his favorite color. His finished drawings tended to be more lines than masses of color. He called them roads seen from an airplane, "You know, like maps."

He spent long periods sitting on the edge of the sandbox, filling pie tins slowly, deliberately patting the surface with the shovel. He handled the sand musingly, letting it drip through his fingers, seeming to enjoy its sensory quality. He sometimes used it for pretend food.

Blocks were his favorite play material. He said he liked them "because you can make so many different things with them." He had a neat and orderly way of building. He built precisely and imaginatively. His constructions were varied in design, and always functional. He made houses, garages, stores, railway stations, tracks, and signals. At first these were solitary ventures, but as he felt surer of himself and the people and the place, he became able to reach out and share his ideas in dramatic play with other children. He became the "light and telephone fixer"; he delivered groceries and furniture and people. He was no longer a solitary doer and viewer. He was a contributing member of his group and he knew it and felt good about it.

The transformation of David from a solemn silent statue of a child to a more freely participating and communicating member of the group did not "just happen." It came about as the result of his teacher's understanding, and her continuous and patient efforts to help him to dare to be more assertive. She began by accepting David's pattern of passive resistance. She did not expect to convert it into a totally different design. But she hoped she could help him to feel more comfortable about himself. She helped him to make connections with other children. She encouraged him to use the play materials. She commended his efforts and shared his satisfaction in small successes. She supported his mild attempts at self assertion. She felt confident that he would enter his next school experience with a degree of assurance that he would not have felt had he not experienced the satisfactions of his preschool year.

David had learned that there are more important things than knowing "hard words." He had learned that ideas can be put into action, that words can be bridges to people, and that feelings can be expressed instead of packaged inside.

He would never become a boldly dashing, assertive person, but nursery school had helped him to take the first steps toward acquiring the self-confidence that provided him with the courage to communicate with others. This had been a major contribution to his personality development.

Trends
in Nursery Education

The current boom of interest in nursery education has focussed public attention on the values of sound preschool experiences for all children, privileged as well as underprivileged. There seems to be increasing acceptance and recognition of the fact that good preschool experiences have value in preparing children for elementary school. Children from economically and culturally deprived environments often start school handicapped in language and communication. They lack backgrounds of experience that stimulate eagerness or even readiness to learn. Many of them begin school marked for failure.

The Head Start program aims at providing enriching preschool experiences for these "culturally disadvantaged" children, experiences which they have missed in their home environments. It also aims to foster positive attitudes toward school and toward learning, through the kind of teaching that captures the child's interest and holds it.

The teacher is clearly the crucial designer and determiner of what goes on in her classroom, whether she is teaching a group of privileged or underprivileged four-year-olds, whether she teaches in a college laboratory school or a day care center. She is a teacher even though she is not engaged in teaching academic subjects. She is actively involved in helping young children to sort out and understand something of the confusions and realities

199

of their three- and four-year-old worlds. She is helping them to have confidence in themselves, and to relate to and trust other selves. She is encouraging them to dare to explore materials and ideas, to ask questions, to seek answers, to know the delights of discovery and success in achievement.

These goals of the preschool teacher are not new, although today they are better understood and more widely respected than in the past. The teacher's role has been influenced by the current goals of nursery educators, and these in turn have been influenced by the current concepts of what is important for children to learn or to be.

There have been recurrent upsurges of interest in preschool education in the United States since the turn of the century when it came to the attention of educators in this country.

Some of these upsurges have been brought about by pressures of social and economic stress. Two world wars and a depression stimulated programs for preschool children on a large scale. Child care centers for children whose mothers were needed in war industry popped up in urban centers. The WPA nursery schools provided care for children of the unemployed as well as employment for unemployed teachers.

Some of these centers were excellent; some were poor and even dangerous. All of them reflected the quality of the teacher and her strengths or weaknesses, her convictions and her caring, or lack of it.

The early nursery schools in this country were strongly influenced by the English nursery or infant schools. The MacMillan sisters had started schools in London for children whose mothers were employed in industry. These schools had a strong social welfare flavor. There was great emphasis on health and cleanliness and physical well-being. The good sisters were trying to make up for some of the lacks of these children's impoverished homes: sunshine, nourishing food, exercise. It was as if the fact that *children have bodies* was the key consideration, and the goal of the educators was to provide the most healthful regime for the best development of these bodies.

Many of the early nursery schools in this country reflected the recognition of this concern for physical welfare. Teachers focussed on maintaining the physical well-being of their children. The routines of washing, toileting, resting, eating, drinking were meticulously observed. Much of the school day was absorbed with the observance of elaborate rituals related to these activities.

In many schools, children were examined by a nurse or physician each morning upon arrival. A quick glance at the throat, nose, skin, hands, chest, greeted each child before he could begin his school day. Records were kept of food intake and refusals, of toileting habits, length of rest, etc.

The function of the teacher during this period of focus on physical welfare was obviously primarily directed to the routines that were involved in developing proper health habits. Much time was spent in the ritualistic practice of hanging up washcloths properly. Cleanliness was not a casual concept. Learning to button and unbutton was high on the list of important goals. Acquisition of sound health habits was a serious business, and the teacher was the constant demonstrator of how to achieve them.

Dr. Gesell, of the Yale Institute for Child Development, added another dimension to teachers' awareness of the physical development and needs of children. His studies revealed an orderly sequence in the development of motor skills. Parents and teachers were informed about "ages and stages" of development, and what to expect at different levels of growing and learning. This was useful as a guide to understanding children, but was also an obstacle when followed too literally. There was danger in labeling children either precocious or retarded if they seemed above or below the expected norm. Dr. Gesell stated that rates of development varied among children, but his readers did not always remember that.

Harriet Johnson, who was one of our pioneers in nursery education, carried the concern for physical well-being in young children a step beyond the concern for proper hygiene, or recognition of "ages and stages" of physical development. She was a strong advocate of recognizing the importance of large muscle development and the need for nursery schools to provide for it. This was in contrast to the stress on fine muscle coordination that was characteristic of kindergarten training at that time. She felt that children needed space in which to move freely, equipment for climbing, big blocks and barrels and boards to lift and carry and build with. This concept was a lively extension of the "children have bodies" notion that had dominated the earlier nursery educators. And it put a new demand on teachers to provide suitable equipment, to encourage its use and to provide safeguards that would insure safe usage. Jungle gyms sprouted in every playground, with a teacher rooted nearby.

Harriet Johnson was also deeply interested in the importance of observing and recording children's behavior, as a way of better understanding their needs. Those of her students who did a full hour "spot" record of a child at work could never again be casual about observing any child anywhere.

Many of our early kindergartens were influenced by European philosophers and educators, Rousseau, Froebel, Pestalozzi, Montessori. The contributions of these people ranged from specific materials like Froebel's "gifts," and Montessori's "didactic materials," to philosophic points of view that children learn most vividly from first-hand, direct experiences rather than second-hand, watered-down interpretations of experience.

Harriet Johnson and Jessie Stanton of the original Bank Street Nursery School were vigorous exponents of the importance of first-hand learning experiences for preschool children. Trips to see the furnace, to watch the coal being delivered, to the stable (to see the horse that delivered the groceries), to the docks, to construction sites—all rich first-hand experiences—were an important part of the curriculum. These plus a rich assemblage of "raw materials" from which children could reconstruct their observations and learning were the chief ingredients of the Bank Street School educational resources.

Paints, clay, crayons and blocks were the raw materials that children used freely with simple "accessory" materials, animals, community and family figures and colored cubes. The work bench provided wood and tools for fashioning the objects needed for more dramatic extensions of block play. In those days there was a noticeable absence of "doll corner" furnishings and toys. Children were encouraged to create their own furniture from hollow blocks and boards.

The trend toward recognizing that children have *minds* as well as bodies presented teachers of these children with new challenges and responsibilities. The teacher was no longer chiefly an overseer and checker of physical fitness. She became an active contributor to children's learning. She recognized that even young children had minds that were eagerly taking in and absorbing impressions of their world, and that they needed to do something about these impressions. They needed "mental jungle gyms," the kinds of experiences that stimulated them to think, and the kinds of play materials that encouraged them to organize their learning in constructive ways. She was tuned toward clarifying and enriching their understanding of their immediate worlds by providing the first-hand experiences which they could then reproduce through use of the raw materials she provided.

A whole new concept of play evolved. Play was recognized as the child's *work*, requiring a total involvement of the child, his mind, energy, motor skill, and purpose. A block was only a block until an *idea* had been added to it, and then it could be anything, a chimney, a barrel, an engine, or a pig.

The teacher's function was not to show and tell, but to provide the opportunities for creative, constructive use of materials, to stimulate thinking. She also assumed responsibility for organizing and arranging the materials for the best possible use. She "set the stage" for the play that made vigorous use of the child's mind as well as his muscles.

Susan Isaacs, in her book *Intellectual Development of Children*,[24] revealed the eagerness with which children seek information and understanding. Her records of the excitement of learning among children in her school are a challenge to teachers to provide similar opportunities for their children.

Jean Piaget, the Swiss research psychologist, contributed insights about the thought processes of children: how they learn, and the meanings they attribute to everyday phenomena; the transitions from intuitive to logical thinking. His chief contribution to the preschool level of teaching was his insistence on the need for providing opportunities for direct experience rather than second-hand telling or showing, and for recognizing the child's level of maturation and readiness for the experience. He also stressed the importance of social interaction, that children often learn more from each other than from the adult teacher. He also emphasized the close association of activity with language in learning. Children learn not only by doing, but by discussion about what they are doing or viewing.

→ Having accepted the facts, first, that young children have *bodies* that are active and growing and deserve opportunities for the best kind of development, and second, that they have *minds* which deserve to be appropriately challenged through experiences and materials that stimulate thought and discovery, the nursery school world finally came to recognize that every young child has *emotions* which influence his learning and relating, as well as his sense of self and competence. Psychoanalytic concepts entered the classroom, and the thoughtful teacher incorporated them into her teaching.

This did not mean that the teacher attempted to become an analyst or deep level interpreter of behavior. It did mean that she acquired an awareness of some of the dynamic principles of emotional development which gave her deeper insights into behavior. She learned about the damage to personality that can be caused by early deprivation and persistent frustration, about the sources of anxiety, and the meaning of aggression and hostility.

Anna Freud, in her observations of English children separated from parents during the war, provided dramatic evidence of the emotional damage sustained by these children. Dr. John Bowlby[11] and Dr. Spitz revealed the injuries to the personality development of infants and young children who were hospitalized or orphaned.

Erik Erikson, anthropologist, psychologist, and writer, in his book *Childhood and Society,*[17] describes the series of critical stages or "central themes" of emotional development through which the individual passes from infancy to adulthood. During infancy the "developmental task" is focussed on acquiring a "sense of trust." The infant experiences this (or he does not) in the relationship with his mother, and it forms a solid (or shaky) base for all future relationships.

The second developmental task is that of acquiring a "sense of autonomy," a sense of assertion of one's self. This is the stage with which preschoolers are still struggling, and for which their teachers need understanding and patience.

This trend of recognizing the importance of feelings as influencers and even determiners of young children's behavior opened a whole new world to their teachers. They became alerted to the fact that emotions affect behavior, that the happy, satisfied child is free to relate, dares to experiment, can endure mistakes or failure or frustration, while the child disturbed by fear and anxiety is unable to live harmoniously with other people, or even with himself. His sense of trust is weak and his sense of autonomy is often distorted. His self image is confused; he may have an excessively low estimate of himself and retreat into passivity, or he may resort to hostile aggressive behavior to convince himself that he can manage his world.

This new awareness of the importance of young children's emotional behavior gave us clues about their needs, and presented new teaching challenges. Teachers were helped to accept the fact that children need to express their feelings as well as to begin to learn controls. Teachers became less critical of behavior which had annoyed them, and tried to discover its causes. They were able to accept some of the less attractive kinds of behavior; they understood the child's need for it, tried to help him to understand it. "I know how you *feel*" was heard in classrooms throughout the nursery school world. "But I can't let you do it," added the teacher, when the action was dangerous to another child or to the child himself.

The recognition that young children have strong feelings which need expression rather than repression or denial sometimes resulted in chaotic over-permissive classrooms, where the teacher allowed total expressiveness without regard for the child's equally strong need for reasonable limits that control and protect.

Teachers must provide these controls, not with threats, punishment, or ridicule, but with clarity and decisiveness about what is essential for reasonable, harmonious group living. This involves having a set of simple "rules," aimed at helping children to acquire self-control. Teachers learned that children were not inhibited by such rules. They seemed to enjoy them and take pleasure in following them.

In summarizing, along with the awareness of children's physical, mental, and emotional development, and their influence on teaching, there has been an increasing trend toward recognizing the *whole* child rather than his parts. Every child has a body, a mind, and feelings which influence his potential for satisfactory adjustment. He also has a family, and he lives in an environment that has social and economic assets or hazards that will influence his success. The teacher of young children must be alert to all of these influences, and thereby be more understanding and more ready to accept the unique individuality of each child and his needs. This understanding is an essential preliminary toward trying to meet these needs.

Madame Montessori: Her Goals and Methods

The current terrible urge to learn more and learn it faster and earlier has influenced parents and educators to examine techniques and philosophies that seem to implement this program of educational speed-up. The pressure has affected all levels of education and is even beginning to seep into the preschool level. J. McV. Hunt, of the University of Iowa, writes, "We drive ourselves and our children in furious pursuit of a distant goal and do not sufficiently treasure the process of getting to the goal which is the essence of education."

The Montessori method of teaching seems to offer one of these promises of quick and early learning. Madame Montessori states that "by teaching children what they need to know early in life, they may be better able to cope with the problems of their culture than by learning later the basic rules when little time is alloted for their mastery."

Parents find it hard to resist magazine cover headlines that shout a message that three-year-olds can be taught to read. Some parents find the order and quiet of Montessori classrooms very appealing, in contrast to the seeming disorder, clutter, and confusion of less organized classrooms.

Some educators have felt that Madame Montessori's success in teaching slum children in Rome has lessons for them in teaching children from "culturally deprived" situations. They feel that her methods and materials may be particularly suited to this group, and some of them may be.

However, before we unconditionally accept and apply her methods, I think we need to review them critically and thoughtfully. Let us ask and try to answer some questions about Madame Montessori. What did she preach and practice? What are the advantages and limitations of her method? To what extent are her methods applicable to our present day educational scene?

Madame Montessori was one of Italy's first women physicians. She combined the discipline of medicine and a genuine scientific attitude with tremendous intuitive gifts, and an equally sincere interest in the welfare and education of young children.

At one point in her career she became directress of the Orthophrenic school in Rome. Children in this school had been diagnosed as idiots. However, Madame Montessori was able to teach them to read and write so that they were capable of passing the Roman public school examination. Her success convinced her that normal children should be capable of learning a great deal more than was customarily expected of them.

She also organized what was probably the forerunner of our modern day care center, her Casa dei Bambini, or children's house in the San Lorenzo slum district of Rome. Here, in what she called "the prepared environment," children learned through manipulation of the "didactic apparatus" which she had devised to teach specific skills and relationships. First, let us look at the materials. Each had a specific teaching function. There were devices to teach color matching, differentiation of sounds, sizes, shapes, textures, weights. Many of them utilized one of Madame Montessori's basic principles, the systematic use of sensory-motor experience as a way of training the sense organs.

Madame Montessori believed that "things are the best teachers," things that subtly develop the child's ability to see, feel, discriminate among varieties of shapes, sounds, textures, etc. The teacher, or "directress" as she prefers to call her, is merely the instrument by which the "things" (didactic materials) are presented to the child. The directress demonstrates the proper usage, then retreats into the background. She steps in only to discourage misuse of materials.

The didactic apparatus seems to fall into four sets of categories. The first group teaches specific differences in size, color, weight, etc. The second group consists of geometric insets which the child traces, then fills in with pencil strokes. This is an exercise aimed at preparing the child to learn to write by acquiring the skill of handling the pencil correctly, and making the strokes which lead to eventual writing.

The sandpaper letters serve a similar function. The child, by tracing the letter with his forefinger and pronouncing the sound of the letter, is undoubtedly establishing some kind of connection between or among his sensory motor tracts. He is seeing, touching, moving, hearing, and thereby reinforcing the experience through these visual, tactile, auditory, and motor paths.

The fourth category of the didactic materials are the teaching frames, designed to teach specific manual skills. There is the button frame, which teaches the technique of buttoning, snap frames, hook-and-eye frames, lacing frames, and now, of course, zipper frames.

Madame Montessori's "prepared environment" consisted of rooms organized for *work* not play. The didactic materials were placed in orderly fashion within reach of the children. There were small chairs and tables which could be moved about, as well as individual floor mats. In addition to the didactic apparatus, materials and objects appropriate for exercises in "practical life tasks" were also part of the planned environment. Some of these tasks were: learning to stand up quietly, learning to place the chair into the table quietly, learning to open and shut a door quietly, learning to scrub a table correctly, to polish brass objects, to polish one's shoes, to carry precious objects, to serve soup from a tureen. It is interesting to note the emphasis on quietness. In her famous "Methods" book Madame Montessori states: "The cultivation of silence is the fruit of a young child's self-mastery."[35]

The creation of these materials and the design of the "prepared environment" were based on Madame Montessori's belief and conviction that from birth to the age of six, the child has "an absorbent mind that endows him with a great capacity for disciplined work and a voracious appetite for learning."[35] She held that the years from three to six are a particularly sensitive period, which should not be allowed to be wasted. In fact, she urgently demanded that these sensitive periods should be exploited, in a positive educational sense, of course.

She also felt that the child's mind develops from within, that in the child's nature as given at birth there is contained in some unique sense all that the child is to become, that we must tend the child as the gardener tends the plant, assured that the natural environment will properly guide its own process of unfolding. Madame Montessori wrote, "The child is a body which grows and a soul which develops. We must neither mar nor stifle the mysterious powers which lie within these two forms of growth, but must await from them the manifestations which we know will succeed one another." [35] "If any education is to be efficacious, it will be only that which tends to help toward the unfolding of the child's individuality." [35]

Madame Montessori was a sincere and dedicated educator. She made a major contribution to the educational thought and practice of her time. Many of her principles are valid today, and many nursery schools make use of her materials, even though they do not consider themselves followers or disciples of their creator.

Her belief that even young children are capable of learning, and that they *are* learning, is a concept we cannot dispute. We believe that very young children will learn either what benefits them, harms them, or confuses them, according to the nature of the teaching environment.

We would agree with Madame Montessori's insistence on the importance of the "prepared environment." Every school or preschool situation has its own individual prepared environment which is influenced by the particular set of "importances" held by those sponsoring the school. Each "prepared environment" is composed of the space itself, the objects, materials, and equipment within the space, and the teacher who guides and assists the children in the use of the space and that which is in it.

Obviously there are great variations in all of these components of any educational experience. The space may be airy, cheery, bright, and spacious, or it may be cramped, gloomy, disorderly, even dirty. The objects and materials in the space may be appealing, attractive, meaningful, arranged to issue invitations to explore and discover and enjoy, or they may be scattered, tattered, dismal, meaningless objects, or materials with limited, rigid uses. The people—the teachers—may be respecting, enjoying, sharing insights, caring about each child's needs and gifts, or controlling, dictating, demanding, limiting each child's individual design of growing and learning.

We would certainly agree with Madame Montessori's belief in the importance of the prepared environment in influencing and even determining the kind of educational experience offered to the children it serves.

We would also agree with her belief in the importance and effectiveness of utilizing the child's sensory-motor impulses as aids in learning. Not just what the child hears, but what he sees, touches, and feels, contribute to his learning. He learns kinesthetically as well as intellectually.

The self-corrective aspect of Montessori's materials is also a valid concept. There is undoubtedly great satisfaction to the child who successfully masters a task which has only one correct way of being completed, or in a sequence that is correctly followed. Inset puzzles have this characteristic, and many of our modern manipulative materials offer this kind of successful completion challenge to our children.

We would not dispute the value of offering "practical life task" experiences to young children. However, we need to be sure that they are meaningful to the children as well as related to their own life experiences.

My criticism of the Montessori application of this principle lies largely in the artificiality of its focus on ritual and mastery of a technique, rather than on delight in the process and in completion of a task that needs doing. I suspect that Montessori teachers feel that this is what is happening in their classrooms. However, I have observed too many spotlessly clean tables being scrubbed according to an elaborate ritual of sequential steps, too many highly polished shoes being shined, too many highly shining brass candlesticks being polished according to the properly prescribed routine, to feel that there is validity or even honesty in such rigid and meaningless performances.

I have also watched children in other schools scrubbing and

sponging messy finger-painted tables, sinks, easels, and floors that were spotted with paints, all needing and getting a good clean-up, not according to a routine of sequential steps, but with vigorous, free clean-up motions, the challenge of a real job to be done, and the satisfaction that came in doing it.

I believe that there are limitations in the exclusive use of the didactic materials which Madame Montessori designed to teach specific concepts or relationships of size, space, contour, weight, color, texture, with the assumption that the mastery of these exercises is the only way of preparing for the academic skills which follow.

Hours spent in fingering sandpaper letters will surely result in learning the shape and direction of line through tactile contact. When this is combined with the visual image of the form and the auditory image of its sound, it results in a neat package of sensory impressions that teach that B is B. But I cannot feel that it necessarily hastens the process of reading for all children exposed to this particular method of teaching. I have observed some three-year-olds being drilled in this particular exercise, and their response was not one of delight in achievement, but rather one of boredom and annoyance at being trapped in a situation from which there was no escape and which contained little meaning.

William Hurd Kilpatrick, who was a vigorous progressive educator of the early twentieth century, felt that the didactic materials "afforded but meager diet for normally active children."[36] He added, "While happy childhood knows no stronger or more fruitful impulse than imaginative and constructive play, in the Montessori schools, *playing* with the didactic apparatus is strictly forbidden."[36] In fact, Madame Montessori stated in her book, "If I were persuaded that children needed to play, I would provide the proper apparatus, but I am not so persuaded."[35]

I would agree with Mr. Kilpatrick that concepts of heat, hardness, weight, size, shape, etc., appear in the normally rich experiences of child life, without the need for specifically designed apparatus to teach these concepts. Furthermore, they are often acquired in *play*.

I cannot help feeling that children will learn the skills of buttoning, buckling, and zipping when their muscular coordination is sufficiently developed, when the motivation for learning is sufficiently aroused, and in the everyday opportunities provided by our current button, buckle, and zipper culture.

Another limitation of the didactic materials is the emphasis put upon the correct use of the material. Successful mastery involves a single method or procedure to teach the appropriate lesson for which it was designed. To me this is definitely limiting. It prevents (actually prohibits) any imaginative use, or the delight that comes from discovering and creating different uses of the material. I do not belittle Madame Montessori's belief in the joy of mastery and successful completion of a task, but I believe there is a shining step beyond this, which her limiting concept of *correct* usage of materials does not permit.

I remember observing two-and-one-half-year-olds at the old Harriet Johnson Nursery School, playing with cylindrical solid insets some thirty years ago. At that time, I didn't know these were Montessori materials. I watched the children lift the vari-sized cylinders from their enclosures. Some children worked at replacing the cylinders in the appropriate spaces. One child filled the spaces with colored cubes, then pushed the frame across the floor with soft chugging sounds. The frame had become a train. I suspect that in a strictly Montessori set-up, this would not have been permitted, since it would be construed as an inappropriate use or misuse of the material. To me, it represented an imaginative and therefore extended use of the material, and one which obviously brought satisfaction to the child. He had been free to elaborate the original material and thereby create new relationships and meaning.

Related to limiting the use of materials by the rigid pattern of a single correct usage is the minor place accorded to creative materials and opportunities for aesthetic experiences. In strictly Montessori schools, music experiences are limited primarily to tone matching or note reading; art materials for free expression are limited and frequently nonexistent. In a Montessori school where I visited recently, there were no blocks, no easels or paints, no clay, no materials for cutting, pasting, or collage. There was no room for these materials, because all of the space was occupied with the didactic teaching materials, and quite obviously they were not considered to be a necessary part of the educational "prepared environment." The only child among 40 children whom I observed engaged in a free, unstructured, nondidactic situation was a little girl struggling to hold inch-long broken bits of crayons with which she was trying to color a 5″ by 7″ scrap of paper. This observation conveyed something of the lack of respect which this school accorded materials other than the official teaching materials. I feel that this represents a serious lack.

My final criticism of the Montessori system is its apparent ignorance or disregard of the importance to young children of being able to act out strong feelings of fear, anxiety, anger, and delight. The only feeling that seems to be recognized and accepted is that of satisfaction in the correct and successful completion of a specific task. Little opportunity and no encouragement is given for social interaction, or for dramatic play as a means of releasing tension and learning through identification and role-playing.

I believe this to be a serious omission. I cannot believe that the satisfaction gained from successful execution of the button board or the correct tracing of a geometrical inset will wipe out or adequately take care of a child's troubled feelings of fear, anger, or rejection. It may be good training in ignoring or covering up strong feelings, but this is hardly a healthy procedure.

In the Montessori system there is little recognition of the importance of learning about living with each other. Social interaction is minimal, limited to occasional help given by one child to another in solving a specific problem. This is permitted, but there is no room for vigorous give and take that healthy preschoolers deserve to experience, and through which they learn reasonable rules of conduct, as well as a growing understanding of themselves.

I feel sure that all serious educators would agree that Madame Montessori made an original and important contribution to her times and culture. Her methods and materials were particularly suited to the mentally defective children for whom they were originally devised. They were and still are effective aids in teaching physically handicapped children, especially the deaf and the blind. However, they seem only partially suited to the multiple needs of today's eager-to-live-and-learn children.

After teaching and observing young children for the past thirty years, I cannot help believing that the child who is ready to read will learn to read without the elaborate preliminaries provided by the Montessori system. The same child will learn to shut a door, or zip a zipper, or clean a table without instruction in the rituals of seventeen to forty-seven sequential steps to be followed and mastered for proper execution of these skills.

Let us use and value the parts of Madame Montessori's principles and methods that make sense to us today, but let us not make a cult of her or her method. Let us be aware of the limitations, and fill in the gaps with some of the knowledge of the dynamics of early childhood to which Madame Montessori had not been exposed.

Surely we can agree with her that "Until early education is made respectable in its own right, and not merely 'readiness' for the supposedly real education which begins at six, there will be a continued waste of human potential and a corresponding need to build into existing school programs more remedial than preventive aspects."[35] Although the teachings of Montessori alone cannot accomplish these goals, they provide one adjunct toward realizing the ideal all preschool teaching seeks.

Teaching the
Disadvantaged Child

The explosion of interest in providing good preschool programs
for children from economically and culturally deprived homes
has been dramatically presented to the American public in the
appearance of Head Start programs throughout the country.
Nursery education has suddenly spurted. It is estimated that
Head Start programs across the country served at least 625,000
young children in its first summer. Some of these programs were
continued into the regular school year, with the promise of continued expansion through increased federal and state funds supporting poverty programs.

The Head Start programs, providing eight weeks of enrichment for children born in poverty, captured the imagination
and enthusiasm of educators of young children. Many of them
spent their summers in sponsoring, setting up, advising, teaching in this massive attempt to develop programs for young
children that would compensate for the deprivation these children had suffered because of the wretched conditions of the
home and community life into which they had been born. Pro-
fessionals from other fields, social workers, psychologists, teachers of older children, teen-age and older volunteers, parents and
other untrained helpers were called upon to join the massive
effort to create and maintain centers for these deprived children.

Nell Goldsmith, who was Chief of the Division of Day Care

in New York City for many years, made the statement that "the success or failure of a program depended primarily on the nursery school teacher. Hers was the key role. Her primary concern for the children and their parents, her ingenuity and inventiveness in providing for their needs, her awareness of the role of each adult participant, her willingness to give and take, were the prime factors in her success." So it would seem that again it is the teacher who determines the nature and quality of experience which is offered to young children in a preschool setting whether it is culturally deprived or enriched.

What should this teacher know about the special needs of children from deprived backgrounds? To what extent is her knowledge of children from more privileged backgrounds applicable to the teaching of these less privileged children? Are there child needs that are unrelated to economic opportunities or lack of them? Does the teacher find that she has different feelings for children from deprived families than she has for children of more affluent families? Does she tend to lump all disadvantaged children into one stereotype of scarred children, injured by their unfortunate life circumstances, whom she will rescue and restore? Or will she discover that even children from poverty have distinct personalities, that some of them have managed to survive the deprivations they have experienced, and that each one deserves to be considered as an important individual?

In discussing what Barbara Biber, Distinguished Research Scholar, Bank Street College of Education, calls the "basic life deficits" of most of these children, I shall borrow many of her thoughts which she presented in two lectures filmed for Project Head Start.

The first "deficit" she describes is the one most commonly discussed: the lack of language skills usually expected at this stage of development. She says that not only is the language immature, but also the "thought processes" which are expressed in language. These children frequently do not know the names of things. Their information is limited.

These language deficits are understandable when one realizes the restricted life experiences of these children. Some of them have never been off the street on which they live. In many of their families there is little conversation; there are no books or newspapers. Many of these homes provide no toys or materials which stimulate experimenting and communication. This restricted use of language, as well as exposure to language, accompanied by lack of experience with materials and activities, constitutes a major obstacle when the child eventually encounters the necessity of learning to read and write.

Dr. Biber points to a "deficit" in the lives of these children which may be even more damaging than meagerness of language. She thinks it is likely that the people with whom the child lives may not only fail to use language freely, but that they may also not be "in close touch with each other as people; that the child hasn't been noticed as the particular person he is; that adults haven't played with him much; that he hasn't been involved in the kinds of connections with people . . . that help him to know who are the familiar people, who are the strange people."[8]

This lack of "connecting with people, of being sensed as a person by other people, of being involved in many rich and important and varied kinds of relationships with the human beings with whom one lives, produces not only a limitation of and deterrent to spoken language in the home, but it acts as a deterrent to learning in general."[11] It is through the "active relationships with people, it is through being known and felt and understood as a person that the child's basic curiosity and interest in the world begins to flower and develop."

Dr. Biber goes on to state that the third deficit is the most serious one of all. She reminds us that these are children "who cannot be sure of basic necessities: Will there be enough food? Is there somebody to take care of me?" She asks, "Is there anybody that really cares about the child in a deep and important way?"

"The basic needs of the very young child to be sure that somebody cares about him and wants him and will take care of him are (often) not fulfilled for these children. In the disturbed family lives in which they find themselves, the world is one of unpredictable threats. The parents, living under extreme conditions of stress and disturbance, do not represent consistent figures for the child. The child may be hit or punished or de-

prived when there is no connection in fact with something that
he has done. He may simply be the innocent subject of the dis-
placed panic of parents. This means that the whole unpredictable world of the child carries a threat with it, and everybody
who comes into his world is naturally suspect, instead of
trusted."[8] She adds that the psychological uncertainty of such
a way of life is often reinforced by disorder in the physical environment which is understandably characteristic of highly disturbed and deprived family situations.

Dr. Biber concludes that these major "deficits of poverty of
language, thought and experience, of minimal human relationships, of threatening, uncertain, unordered life environment"[8]
are major diminishers of the development of personality at its
very roots.

The teacher who is convinced that these deficits are deterrents
to healthy, productive personality development will then be
ready to consider the extent to which a good preschool program can begin to fill in these desperate lacks. These teachers
are already clear in their belief that what happens to children
in the early years of life is basic and important for all the rest
of the years to come. How they learn, what ideas they get about
people and the world in which they live, as well as how they
feel about themselves, are all based on their preschool experiences.

Dr. Biber makes the important point that although children
from disadvantaged areas will need certain special understanding, certain special adjustment to their particular needs and
characteristics, they are fundamentally like all other children.
"They have the same potentialities, the same curiosity, the same
basic human problems to face in life, except that life has given
them some extra ones that no children really should have."[9]
She feels that their needs are not dissimilar to those of more
advantaged children; they are more intense.

Our disadvantaged children have been denied the opportunity
of having their normal sense of curiosity developed and stimulated. They have had little opportunity to deal with the world
of ideas. Their natural interest in knowing where things come
from, what they are called, how they change, has not been met
by answers or experiences that would satisfy or stimulate further

questions. Their opportunities to explore the physical world have been similarly limited, with a consequent lack of opportunity to develop physical controls, skills and coordination, or to know themselves as persons who have these skills. Their knowledge of the nature of their physical world is equally limited. They have had limited experiences in problem solving, in the satisfactions that come from being able to accomplish a simple task. They have missed the opportunity to become sensitive observers of the world of shapes, sounds, textures, size, color, etc.; in fact they are likely to be poor (because unpracticed) observers. They have lacked opportunities to do and make things that bring satisfaction and a sense of mastery and skill. They have been denied the opportunity to develop constructive skills that will give them a feeling that they can produce something positive rather than destructive. They have had little if any opportunity to dramatize or symbolize or reproduce the meaning of their experiences through play, as more advantaged children are encouraged to do.

Dr. Biber stresses the fact that the dramatic play in which preschoolers engage so freely is one of the important ways in which they gain knowledge about themselves and their world. They "rehearse what they realize. In their pretending, they are free of reality, they can make things appear to be the way they really are not; they can express wishes; they can express feelings that could not be expressed legitimately in their real relationships in life. They set themselves problems, they solve problems. They take roles, they act like grown-ups, they act like babies, they get sick, get well, die and come to life again. They rehearse the knowledge they have gained about the real world. They are trainmen, engineers, pilots and firemen. The whole panorama of life is lived over again in the play of children." Dr. Biber concludes that "if there is any way of gaining knowledge that is particularly suitable to this stage of development, it is in the play which they spontaneously devise, but which *needs nevertheless an attentive and understanding teacher for its support and nourishment.*"[9] [my italics] This our disadvantaged children have never had.

They have had no practice in developing conceptual order in their world of things. Not only are they unclear about the uses and functions of many objects, they do not know their names. They are unaware of relationships or grouping of objects or events, or that some things can change from one thing into another. Their concept of organization of events in time is also limited.

The challenge presented to the teacher in meeting the multiple deficits of these children is a tremendous one, one which demands deep reserves of understanding, patience, courage and strength. She needs skills and techniques that will aid her in teaching, but she also needs the kind of warmth that will permit children to dare to relate to her, and to trust her. Her goal is to help these children to see themselves and to feel themselves as people who are cared for, who are worthwhile, who are capable of doing and mastering things, who can communicate with other children and adults, who can believe in their ability to initiate activities, who can enjoy and learn and play.

How does she go about achieving these goals? I cannot give a blueprint for teaching these children, but I shall try to make a few suggestions of ways to extend their horizons. First, it would seem reasonable that in helping children to acquire skills in language and thinking, to become better talkers, we need to listen to them, listen hard, try to understand them even when their words or pronunciation is difficult to understand. This is one way of helping them to become listening people. We cannot expect them to sit down in an orderly way and listen attentively to a story. Showing pictures, talking about them, asking the children to talk about them are appropriate preliminaries to group story-reading times.

Probably more effective than exercises in naming objects or describing pictures is the stimulus to language and communication that comes from free spontaneous play activities among children themselves. A toy telephone demands that children speak into it to communicate something to somebody. A fireman intent on putting out a fire needs to communicate with the tenants, "Where da fire?," and with his fellow firemen, "Bring da hoses, git da ladder!"

Basic to the development of language and thought is the need to begin extending and widening the child's limited background of experiences through trips to neighborhood places of interest: a grocery store to buy fruit or vegetables or snacks, a garage or gas station, a fire station, a post office, a shoe repair shop. The teacher's interest in these places, the questions she raises, the observations to which she alerts the children, all stimulate language and understanding. These first-hand experiences also provide substance for dramatic play, for representation in various play materials which in turn demand verbal accompaniment.

The teacher poses questions as a way of stimulating thinking and observation. "Do you need two blocks or three blocks to finish your gas station?" "How many crackers do we need?" "How many boys are here today?" "How many girls?" "What color is Nancy's dress?" "How can we make Roger's building more steady?" "What did we see at the grocery store that was red?" "What moves fast?" "What moves slowly?"

Opposed to the theory of teaching language through extending horizons, and encouraging the verbalizing of first-hand experiences, is the point of view held by professors Carl Bereiter and Siegfried Engelman of the University of Illinois.[5] These two men feel very strongly that the language deficit of the disadvantaged child is his central handicap, and the one from which many others derive. Since academic success in school is so dependent on language skills, and since the disadvantaged children are so lacking in these skills, they believe it is essential to focus the training of these preschool children on strictly academic objectives. They maintain that since these children are so far behind middle-class children, the educational process must be speeded up to help them catch up in the acquisition of academic skills.

Bereiter and Engelman do not feel that traditional nursery school practices are suited to provide the rapid learning that is essential for this "catching up" process. Accordingly, they recommend radical departures from established practices of early childhood educators. They believe that "direct instruction" through intensive drill in language and arithmetic is the best preparation for academic learning. They maintain that their method of teaching through repetitious insistent drill at high speed does not result in excessive strain or anxiety in children. They admit that their highly structured teaching does not encourage or even permit creativity and self-expression, nor does this concern them.

They maintain that there is no need for a close affectionate relationship between the teacher and the child; rather the teacher-child relationship should be characterized by shared intellectual interests. They state that the effective teacher is one whose major interest is in making children more intellectually competent. Such a teacher is confident that he can make children do what he wants them to do. He is not particularly concerned with the individuality of each child. He rewards (with cookies or raisins, handshakes and praise) the children who "try"; he punishes (with isolation, withholding of cookies, shaking or slaps) the children who exhibit undesirable behavior, who do not try.

Their "motivational bridges" of cookies and raisins remind me of the methods used in some of the infant schools in England which provided care for the children of mothers who were needed in industry during the early days of the industrial revolution. One ingenious teacher devised alphabet cookies that were awarded to the children who learned to recite the alphabet correctly. Those who could not do so were denied the cookies, of course.

Bereiter and Engelman present evidence of the success of the intensive drill method in their program of cognitive stuffing, in the increased I. Q. scores of their subjects. I do not challenge the veracity of their charts and figures. We know that intensive repetitious drill can result in certain kinds of measurable direct learning. What is not so measurable are the possible secondary results of exposure to such rigidly imposed exercises: submission to the adult authority, fear of failure or reprisal, lack of confidence, lack of curiosity, deprivation of opportunities to discover and explore.

Lois Barclay Murphy, of the Menninger Foundation, in a letter to the New York Times, stated, "cognitive stimulation involves more than the capacity to use sentences." She reminds us that there are other cognitive functions to be nourished, such as curiosity, reflectiveness, problem-solving, and that these are acquired through active play—with blocks, with plastic materials, through field trips, cooking, gardening, and the discussions stimulated by these activities. She adds that the "individual relation and identification of the young child with his teacher is perhaps most basic to learning to want to learn."

Bereiter and Engelman will undoubtedly attract a flurry of followers who will accept their approach and emphasis on concentrated drill. However, those teachers who are concerned with the healthy development of the whole child will not be satisfied with an approach that focusses on only one aspect of his development. This does not mean that these teachers are unaware of the need to provide the kind of order in the classroom that will encourage learning.

Dr. Biber reminds us that there are certain practical aspects to teaching these children of which teachers should be aware. She urges us to realize that these children are not accustomed to the regulated, orderly life of more privileged children. She feels that one of the most important things we can do is to have things very clear, very simple, very well-organized. "In these rooms there should be no higgledy-piggledy piling up of things. The schedule should be clear." The children should be helped to understand the sequence of the daily program, what follows what. In presenting new materials or activities, the teacher needs to be very concrete, very specific, very simple. In demonstrating what she means, she should not rely too heavily on verbal explanations. "The goal should be to build a world for them in the classroom that is a clear world, one in which they know where things are, what's going to happen next, and have a set of clear expectations that they can count on."[8]

Many teachers who have worked for the first time with disadvantaged children have been surprised to find that these children often seem indifferent to the play materials. They pick them up, discard them, or destroy them. This is understandable when one realizes that few of these children have had experiences of possessing or valuing toys. They have had no experience in caring for things. Many of them haven't been cared for themselves. It takes time to acquire a caring attitude towards objects or even toward other children or adults. They need active demonstrations from the teacher both in being cared for by her, and in ways of caring for things, possibly through special programs of mending, fixing, cleaning, etc.

Teachers have also discovered that they need to take a more active role in playing with these disadvantaged children. Although the teacher's goal is to steer children into discovering the delights of free play, she realizes that in the beginning, they may need more active guidance than she is usually accustomed to give. She may do more talking about what materials a child needs, or what his building plans are, or help him to join the play of other children.

Teachers have also found that these children may seem subdued and distant in the beginning. They may even seem suspicious of adults. Again, this involves understanding and patience on the part of the teachers. Why should these children trust and love you just because you confront them with a place and things and yourself as a dispenser of pleasure and understanding? Don't try to move in too fast on these children. They need time to savor the situation, to look and listen. They need to observe and assure themselves that these are grownups who are dependable and caring. They need demonstrations that they are respected by these new adults. They need to experience the support, clarity, and affection offered by this new teacher person until they dare to believe they can trust her not to change or disappear.

As these children begin to see and feel themselves as cared-for people, who are worthwhile in the eyes of teachers, they will dare to relate, even to make mistakes, because they will not fear reprisals. They will come to experience the comfort and security of controls that safeguard their wild impulses to hurt and destroy. They will be safe with adults who protect them from their own angry feelings and who help them to learn better ways of handling their hostility, anxiety and fear.

They will learn that learning is hard, but also exciting and fun. They will be readier to face with confidence the next step in learning at school.

Nell Goldsmith says that "No one needs to 'wind up' these young children or put pressure on them to make them curious, or to push them to learn. They ask only the opportunity, a stimulating environment, companionship, responsive and responsible guidance. "And it is the teacher who is the crucial one who helps these children to develop a positive self-image, to know their unique importance, to gain independence, cope with problems, relate to their peers and their adults, improve their skills and enjoy life."

This is a goal much broader than merely offering an organized and reasonably orderly program of stimulation to compensate for their cognitive deficits. Teachers must not make the mistake of focussing primarily on language, concept formation, and perceptual discrimination. Their chief focus must be on the child and the development of his self image. The child who feels good about himself will be eager to learn, and he will feel confidence in his ability to learn. It is the teacher who can give or withhold this gift.

Goals and Roles
of the Teacher

In these pages I have tried to present live children, parents, and teachers. I have quoted their words, described their actions and interactions, as well as their feelings about themselves and each other. My chief focus has been on the teacher: how her teaching reflects what she knows, and the kind of person she is.

I have tried to describe the kind of teaching that will help young children to gain confidence in themselves as learners, communicators, "doers." Children fortunate enough to experience this kind of teaching will be readier for whatever comes next in their educational experience, because they have been permitted and encouraged to be themselves, and to learn how those selves work and learn. They will have acquired more than skills and techniques; they will have acquired attitudes toward learning that will influence all the rest of their schooling. They will have been encouraged to ask questions, to seek answers, and to discover the wonders of the everyday world around them. They will have learned that a teacher is a person to be trusted, and they will have felt her respect for them.

Parents of these children have also benefited from their exposure to this kind of teaching. They have had the opportunity of becoming more enlightened about what young children are like and what they need. They also become more tolerant, more patient, less demanding, less guilty about their own lack of understanding. The result of this is that as their concerns diminish, their enjoyment increases. I have watched the faces of parents changing from expressions of grim, critical disapproval to smiling delight and pride, as they watch their children.

"I never thought Anthony would be able to skin the cat," commented one father as he watched his son demonstrating his newly learned trick.

"I wasn't aware that Sonya had such a flair for painting. Look at those lovely colors! I'm going to frame it and hang it in our bedroom."

"I've stopped nagging Donna," reported her mother. "I realize I was expecting her to act like a seven-year-old. She's only four. She's like a new child, or maybe she's the same, but I never took time to recognize her. She really is a darling. We have such fun together. I'm glad I found out in time."

What about the teacher herself? What are her goals, her convictions, her concerns? How does she see her role? What are her strengths, her needs, her limits, her hopes? What does she need to be—and *not* be?

First of all, she believes in the importance of nursery education as a crucial influence on the educational experiences which follow it. She believes that the preschool years are ones in which basic foundation patterns of learning are laid. She believes in constantly assessing her own methods, and in increasing her understanding. She is alert to current research and the findings of other related disciplines, and welcomes knowledge that will deepen her understanding of children and their needs.

She sees herself as someone who reflects current knowledge and insights about what is important in the education of young children. She is not "taken in" by everything she reads or hears, but she does not close the door to new or challenging ideas.

The teacher of young children needs to have an organized reservoir of knowledge about what children are like, how they grow, their stages of development, what they seem to need, how they learn, as well as something about the nature of the world in which these children are trying to learn. She needs to be aware of some of the obstacles to effective learning, and how she, as a teacher, can help overcome them. She needs to know how much she doesn't know, as well as when to seek help from other disciplines. She needs to be constantly open to new insights and new discoveries that will aid her in her search for increased understanding of children's needs and the ways in which she may most effectively meet them in her teaching.

But along with knowing, she needs to be the kind of person who can put knowledge to work in ways that will make sense to children, as well as bring pleasure and satisfaction to her as a teacher. She needs to know how to communicate with children; she also needs to know when to be quiet.

This teacher is clear about what she is *not*. She is not a magician, although she knows that effective teaching can often change the lives of young children and their parents. She knows this is not achieved by magic. She cannot make a hawk into a dove by wishing. She also knows that she is neither omniscient nor omnipotent. She knows that there are many things she doesn't know, and many things she can't do. She is willing to admit her lacks and frailties. She knows she is not a therapist, although as a teacher, she may be collaborating in an educational situation that in itself has therapeutic values. She does not try to be a deep level interpreter of behavior although she may point out consequences of certain kinds of behavior as well as seek logical reasons for it.

If these are some of the things that the teacher is *not*, we must also review some of the things that she *is*.

First, she is a "stage-setter," an invitation-extender. She organizes the space and the materials in it, in ways that will invite active experimenting, discovery and learning. She also sets the tone, the atmosphere which encourages this learning. She expects it to be lively and enjoyable.

She is a reasonable setter of limits. She protects children by not permitting them to do things that might endanger themselves or others. She discourages misuse of materials. She is clear without needing to be punitive. She says, "I won't let you hurt other people. I won't let other people hurt you." "Hammers are for pounding nails at the workbench, not for pounding furniture." And she means it. She helps children to accept the limits that safeguard, and to begin to incorporate their own controls.

She helps children face reality. She knows the intensity of

feelings that young children have, and the pain they suffer when frustrated. She accepts the feeling, but also tries to help the child accept the reality of not always being able to have or do or be what he wants.

"I know it's hard not to ride the new bike when you want it. But the next turn will be yours." Part of her role as "sympathetic reality facer" is also that of "clarifier and connection-maker."

"It made you angry when I took the big stick away from you. But it was just too dangerous. I couldn't let you hurt other children with it."

She is a casual and impartial revealer and supporter of what *is*. When Keith asks, "How come girls sit down and boys stand up when they go to the toilet?," she answers, simply and directly, "Because girls aren't made like boys." She may follow this up later by pointing out the obvious anatomical difference that makes sitting or standing an appropriate mode of toileting. She is neither shocked nor embarrassed by the direct question. She is neither devious nor overwhelming in her response. She accepts the honesty and directness of the question and replies with similar simplicity and candor.

She is alert to cues that children give her about themselves and their needs, and she is a consistent accepter and respecter of each child's uniqueness. She is not interested in identical responses or products. She respects differences and strives to help each child discover his own particular personality.

The teacher I have been trying to describe is first and finally *herself*. She is aware of her limitations and her strengths. She knows the satisfactions and delights of creative teaching. She feels certain that her teaching will be making a crucial contribution to each child's concept of himself, which will be the best possible foundation for the more formal education which follows the preschool period. She will never be satisfied that she knows enough, and will continuously expose herself to new learning. She will also realize that her children are often her most lively teachers. She will "rejoice, give thanks and sing" that she is a teacher of young children. There is nothing that she would rather be!

Bibliography

1   Almy, Millie Corinne. *Young Children's Thinking.* New York Teacher's College Press, 1966.
2   Association for Childhood Education International. *Basic Propositions For Early Childhood Education.* 1966.
3   Association for Childhood Education International. *Early Childhood: Crucial Years For Learning.* n.d.
4   Baruch, Dorothy. *Parents And Children Go To School.* Scott, Foresman & Co., 1939.
5   Bereiter, Carl and Engelman, Siegfried. *Teaching Disadvantaged Children In The Preschool.* Prentice-Hall, 1966.
6   Beyer, Evelyn. *A New Level In Teacher-Parent Relationships.* National Assn. for the Education of Young Children Bulletin, 1954.
7   Beyer, Evelyn. *Nursery School Settings—Invitation To What?* National Assn. for the Education of Young Children, 1958.
8   Biber, Barbara. *The Educational Needs Of Deprived Children.* University of the State of New York, State Education Dept., 1965.
9   Biber, Barbara. *The Impact Of Deprivation On Young Children.* University of the State of New York, State Education Dept., 1965.
10 Biber, Barbara. *Play As A Growth Process.* New York: Bank Street Publication, n.d.
11 Bowlby, John. *Maternal Care And Infant Health.* Geneva World Health Organization, 1951.
12 Carson, Rachel. *Sense Of Wonder.* Harper & Row, 1965.
13 Chukovsky, Kornei. *From Two To Five.* Berkeley, Calif.: University of California Press, 1963.
14 Christianson, Helen; Rogers, Mary; and Ludlum, Blanche. *The Nursery School: Adventure In Living And Learning.* Boston: Houghton Mifflin Co., 1961.

15   Doman, G. Penn. *How To Teach Your Baby To Read.* New York: Random House, 1964.

16   Fraiberg, Selma. *The Magic Years.* New York: Charles Scribner's Sons, 1959.

17   Erikson, Erik. *Childhood and Society.* New York: W. W. Norton & Co., 1963.

18   Freud, Anna. *Psychoanalysis For Teachers And Parents.* New York: Emerson Books, 1935.

19   Freud, A., and Burlingham, D. *War And Children.* New York: International Universities Press, 1943.

20   Gesell, A. and Ilg, F. L. *Infant And Child In The Culture Of Today.* New York: Harper, 1943.

21   Gross, Dorothy Weissman. "Is Play Obsolete"? *Saturday Review of Literature,* Nov. 16, 1963.

22   Hartley, Ruth; Frank, Lawrence; and Goldenson, Robert. *Understanding Children's Play.* New York: Columbia Univ. Press, 1952.

23   Hymes, James, L. *Effective Home-School Relations.* New York: Prentice-Hall, Inc., 1953.

24   Isaacs, Susan. *Intellectual Growth In Young Children.* London: Routledge & Kegan, Paul, Ltd., 1963.

25   Isaacs, Susan. *Social Development In Young Children.* New York: Harcourt Brace & Co., 1939.

26   Johnson, Harriet M. *Children In The Nursery School.* New York: John Day, 1928.

27   Jones, Marjorie Graham. *A Two Year Old Goes To Nursery School.* National Assn. for the Education of Young Children, 1964.

28   Kilpatrick, W. H. *The Montessori System Examined.* Boston: Houghton Mifflin, 1914.

29   Landreth, Catherine. *Education Of The Young Child.* New York: John Wiley & Sons, 1942.

30   Landeck, Beatrice. *Time For Music. Public Affairs,* pamphlet No. 260, 1958.

31   Law, Norma. *What Are Nursery Schools For?* Washington D.C.: Assn. for Childhood Education International, 1964.

32   Lewis, Claudia. *Children Of The Cumberland.* New York: Columbia, 1946.

33   Lowenfield, Viktor. *Your Child And His Art.* New York: MacMillan Co., 1954.

34   Mitchell, Lucy Sprague. *Here And Now Story Book.* New York: E. P. Dutton & Co., Inc., 1921.

35   Montessori, Maria. *The Montessori Method.* New York: Frederick A. Stokes, 1912.

36   *Montessori In Perspective.* National Assn. for the Education of Young Children, 1966.

37   Moustakas, Clarke E., and Berson, Minnie Perrin. *The Young Child In School.* New York: William Morrow & Co., 1956.

38   Murphy, L. B., and Associates. *Personality In Young Children.* New York: Basic Books, 1956.

39   Murphy, Lois B. *The Widening World Of Childhood.* New York: Basic Books, Inc., 1962.

40   New York State Council for Children. *Good Living For Young Children.* 1960.

41   *Nursery School Portfolio.* Published by Assn. for Childhood Education International.

42   *Packets for Nursery School Teachers.* New York: Bank Street Publications, Bank Street College of Education.

43   Piaget, Jean. *Judgment And Reasoning In The Child.* New York: Harcourt & Brace, 1928.

44   Piaget, Jean. *Language And Thought Of The Child.* Humanities Press, 1959.

45   Read, Katherine. *The Nursery School.* Philadelphia and London: W. B. Saunders Co., 1966.

46   Ruben, Margaret. *Parent Guidance In The Nursery School.* New York: International Universities Press, Inc., 1960.

47   Rudolph, Marguerita. *Living And Learning In The Nursery School.* New York: Harper Bros., 1954.

48   Rudolph, Marguerita, and Cohen, Dorothy. *Kindergarten: A Year Of Learning.* New York: Appleton-Century-Crofts, Inc., 1964.

49   Tarnay, Elizabeth Doak. *What Does The Nursery School Teacher Teach?* National Assn. for the Education of Young Children, 1965.

50   Schulman, Anne Shaaker. *Absorbed In Living, Children Learn.* National Assn. for the Education of Young Children, 1967.

51   Sheehy, Emma. *Children Discover Music And Dance.* New York: Holt, Rinehart & Winston, 1959.

52   Wann, Kenneth; Dorn, M.E.; and Liddle, E.A. *Fostering Intellectual Development In Young Children.* New York: Bureau of Publications, Teachers College, Columbia University, 1962.

SOURCES OF ILLUSTRATIONS

Frontispiece, photograph by Martin Helfer; page 16, photograph by Dana Hurst; page 39, photograph by Lois Barclay Murphy; page 49, photograph by Martin Helfer; page 66, photograph by Martin Helfer; page 87, photograph by Henry E. Brown; page 105, photograph by Martin Helfer; page 111, photograph by Lois Barclay Murphy; page 122, photograph by Mary K. McHugh; page 129, photograph by Dorothy Levens; page 152, photograph courtesy of Sarah Lawrence College; page 170, photograph by Lois Barclay Murphy; page 187, photograph by Lois Barclay Murphy.